WOMEN AND MEN AS LEADERS

WOMEN AND MEN AS LEADERS

In Business, Educational, and Social Service Organizations

TRUDY HELLER
Foreword by Lois Hart

PRAEGER SPECIAL STUDIES • PRAEGER SCIENTIFIC
A J.F. BERGIN PUBLISHERS BOOK

Library of Congress Cataloguing in Publication Data

Heller, Trudy.
  Women and men as leaders.

  Bibliography: p.
  Includes index.
  1. Leadership 2. Executives 3.Women
executives. 4. Executive ability. I. Title.
HD57.7.H44   658.4'092   81-17084
ISBN 0-03-058948-7   AACR2

Published in 1982 by Praeger Publishers
CBS Educational and Professional Publishing
A Division of CBS, Inc.
521 Fifth Avenue, New York, New York 10017 U.S.A.

0123456789   056   987654321

Printed in the United States of America

CONTENTS

To my parents, Sid and Ida Heller,
who didn't believe it

ACKNOWLEDGMENTS

This book is the product of a process which has developed over a period of four years and involved many people. I am grateful to everyone who has provided encouragement, helpful criticism, and essential support services. The leaders and co-workers of the study especially have my respect and appreciation for their courage in allowing me to intrude upon their work lives.

Many friends have encouraged me in this endeavor, including Cathy Moore, Sharon Smith, Barbara Salkin and my Women's Studies colleagues in Colorado, Jan Demarest, Tracy Ehlers, Barbara Parker, and Marcia Weskott. Also among those friends are my in-laws, William and Beatrice Van Til, who provided support and guidance during the writing and publication process. My students and workshop participants have played an important role in this process by challenging me to transform data into useful and meaningful information.

Several people read parts of earlier drafts of the book and provided helpful criticism. I appreciate Linda Smircich, Phyllis Padow, Eric Gnepp, and Joyce Varner for their feedback.

Without the interviewers the project would not have been possible. I am grateful to Bob Culleton, Sylvia Kunreuther, Jean Mayne, Steve Goldberg, and John Mulroy for their assistance in gathering the information that has been the foundation of this book. I am grateful to Gail Maxwell for her competent typing and drafting and for her friendship. I have also depended on Margaret Gnepp and Tina Davidson for typing and drafting respectively. James Bergin has dispelled my negative stereotypes of publishers, and has been a pleasure to work with.

Finally, my family has played an essential role in this project. My husband, John Van Til, has been a tireless source of vision, financial support, and editorial assistance. My babies, Ross and Claire, born during these past four years, have lovingly challenged me to balance my work and family lives.

Trudy Heller

FOREWORD

Leadership is not a new phenomenon, nor are studies of leaders. But fortunately, now there is fresh information available in WOMEN AND MEN AS LEADERS for professionals, of both genders, who want to prepare for new leadership positions or to enhance their effectiveness in positions they currently hold and thereby need to understand the dynamics of leadership and to create their own vision of it.

Trudy Heller's research provides the reader with one more clue in the complex puzzle called leadership. Increasing numbers of women are moving into leadership positions, enjoying their new authority and influence, proving their ability to lead, and eyeing even higher executive roles. Therefore, women need models to emulate. But up until now, most leadership studies excluded women as subjects. At last, we have a comparative study of both genders.

Men are also in transition, re-evaluating the role of work in their lives, and learning new attitudes and behaviors towards their female colleagues. Therefore, men need fresh insights into the study of leadership.

Heller's research provides a unique comparison of pairs of male and female leaders in business, educational, and social service settings. Her method offers us the opportunity to compare the styles of the two genders and to see how leaders differ in these three types of organizations. After reading about these leaders, it was tempting to conclude that leaders in the social services are on the cutting edge of helping us all move toward more androgynous management.

Another difficulty with past research on leadership, besides the lack of female subjects, has been the assumption that the most appropriate model for leadership was male. If this were true, the women moving into leadership had two choices: one was to mold one's behavior and style more like men's, and the other was to reject the traditional model and replace it with a feminine one.

These two alternatives overlooked the possibility of synthesizing the best of both models. Heller reminds us of the limitations of defining effective leadership using stereotypic definitions of masculine and feminine behavior. More suitable is an assessment of how each gender's strengths can contribute to effective leadership.

Visionary future leaders will avoid the trap of rigid stereotypes developed in the past and instead create new images and possibilities. In one case, Heller demonstrates how difficult it is for individual leaders to move out of stereotypic behaviors when their co-workers retain a rigid image of what is most appropriate for each gender.

Who benefits if today's leaders analyze popular beliefs about male and female leadership behaviors? Certainly more than these individuals will; their subordinates, bosses, and colleagues, as well as aspiring leaders, will benefit.

If the ideas presented here are ignored or discounted, we risk a loss of time and productivity and ensure that roles will remain confused. It is time we dispel myths, explore new options, and create a vision of leadership that ensures a more meaningful future.

The process of leading others is fascinating. The dynamics are complex. The rewards for searching for new ways are worth the effort.

Lois B. Hart

PREFACE

I first became aware of my interest in the topic, leadership, when as a twenty-eight year old I took my first professional job and began to work under the supervision of a woman. In the months that followed intense conflict with my boss developed. After two years on the job I resigned one day in a burst of anger.

The disappointment was manifold. My stereotype of the humanistic lady boss was destroyed. My assumption that my professional development would be nurtured by this woman had proven to be false. My notion that an easy flow between work and home life would be facilitated by the woman who was my superior was far from reality. The hope that I might promote "feminist" policies through my position and with the support of my female boss had been dashed.

I emerged from this traumatic experience with a great void in my psyche. In doing battle with my boss I had become aware of my own ambition and desire to lead. Ironically, though, I could not envision a way, a style of leadership that might suit me.

The task of my recovery was to seek a way. Part of my search has taken the forms of study and research—including the leadership study which is the basis of this book. No piece of research has been more personally motivated or more personally satisfying.

The study was originally conducted as a dissertation project at Temple University. It was designed for quantitative analysis of aggregate data. Subjective interview data were gathered merely as a check on the honesty of the information provided by questionnaires. The rationale for conducting the interviews was that on a sensitive topic such as attitudes toward women a live interviewer might be able to elicit more honest and complete information by establishing rapport with the interviewee.

The following is a discussion of the process of locating participants and collecting information for the study.

Subject Search

A goal of the subject search was to develop a sample of leaders who would be as varied as possible in terms of the kinds of organizations they led, age, seniority, marital/family status, race and educational level. The rationale for this goal was the notion that each of these variables related to a cultural context which had everything to do with perceptions of women and men as leaders.

Another goal was to have male-female pairs of leaders who were as well matched as possible on the following criteria:

1) On the organization or kind of organization in which they worked;

2) On the kind of position held in terms of duties and responsibilities;

3) On their organizational rank.

The rationale for this goal was that sex differences would be observed more readily if the leaders were doing the same type of work in the same type of organizational milieu.

The subject search was, perhaps, the most difficult part of the study, and an interesting source of data in itself. For practical reasons the search was limited geographically to the metropolitan areas of two large cities. The search was further refined to people who had direct supervision over at least three subordinates, as the interaction between the leader and subordinates, peers and superiors was the major focus of the study. This restriction disqualified leaders such as a bank vice-president who supervised only a secretary and dealt mainly with customers. Names of potential participants were sought through the following sources:

1) Through consultants and colleagues who knew people in organizational leadership positions through their work.

2) Through personnel officers in organizations.

3) Through associations for women executives, such as the National Association of Bank Women.

Once a potential participant was located through one of these sources and their commitment to be included in the study was secured, they were asked to nominate a matching leader who fit the criteria listed above. Usually a female leader was sought first because she was likely to have several male counterparts as required by the criteria for matching. A male leader, on the other hand, was less likely to have a woman with whom he could be matched. There was, however, no discernible pattern of willingness to participate. Both men and women, as counterpart nominees, declined to participate.

This process of nomination of a matching counterpart of the opposite sex was the only formal hint that the study was about sex roles. In all letters, questionnaires and interviews, the study was simply described as being about "organizational leadership." The purpose of this policy was to avoid getting socially-acceptable and "liberated" responses when the truth was otherwise.

Another criterion of selection developed unintentionally. Only leaders who perceived themselves as fairly successful were willing to participate—although there is variation in success of the twelve participants in terms of how favorably or unfavorably they are viewed by co-workers (including subordinates, peers, superiors) and in terms of career advancement as indicated by the follow-up questionnaire three years after the original data collection (see epilogue). Yet a common reason for declining to participate was a crisis in the workplace for the particular leader in question.

Data Gathering

Once a pair of leaders was located and committed to participating in the study, the following procedure was followed to collect information. First, a list of subordinates, peers and superiors was obtained from the leader. The names in each category—subordinate, peer, superior—were then ranked in random order using a Table of Random Numbers.

Questionnaires were then mailed to the leader, the three highest ranking subordinates, the three highest ranking peers and the one highest ranking superior. When one of the co-workers was unwilling to fill in the questionnaire, another questionnaire was mailed to the next person on the list of randomly ordered names. Hence for each leader who participated in the study, information was available from a sample of three subordinates, three peers and one superior.

Names of a leader and co-worker group were then given to an interviewer. Leaders were assigned to interviewers so that one-half of the female leaders were interviewed by a woman and one-half were interviewed by a man—and the same for the male leaders. I also asked each interviewer whether they felt their sex had an effect on the interview situation. They almost unanimously reported that their gender made no difference. One male interviewer, however, reported that interviewees responded to him as an intermediary for the researcher, a woman.

Ideally, all participants would have been interviewed; however, in cases where peers and superiors were located at some distance from the leader being studied the cost of interviewing was prohibitive. Also, in the case of the university department heads, the superiors declined the invitation to be interviewed.

Treatment of Data

Hence the data from twelve leaders and their subordinates, peers and superiors were treated in aggregate. The interviews were reduced to a "lib" scale, a quantified measure of traditional to liberal attitudes toward women and careers. A series of regression analyses were performed aimed at determining the "best" models for explaining variance in the role legitimation ratings of male and female leaders. Follow-up techniques were then used to determine whether the differences were statistically significant.

Upon completing these analyses, although significant results were found both in the explanatory value of the models of role legitimation for male and female leaders and in the differences between these models (Heller, 1978), I felt that the data had more to offer. I was also concerned, in presenting my results to groups of women and men who cope with the daily demands of leadership, that the statistical analyses did not seem to speak to the people who might make use of the information. Their unanswered questions prompted me to undertake a new type of data analysis—taking the risk that the post hoc nature of the analysis would, in some instances, create a mismatch between the questions being addressed and the type of data used to respond. A comparative case study analysis without regard for statistical significance and with full use of interview material seemed to be an appropriate vehicle for tapping this rich source of information. Hence this book.

Leadership or Sex Roles?

My study of the leadership literature led to the conclusion that while a great number of studies of women in management have been produced in the last decade, this literature exists largely outside the mainstream of leadership thought and theory making. Most of the literature is published in so-called "women studies" journals which have questionable value to the primarily female authors in terms of gaining promotion to positions of leadership in their academic organizations. Most of these studies plug into pre-existing theories most of which were developed through studies of men. In short, the status of the research literature on women in management is similar to the status of women in management—marginal and with only token representation in authoritative places.

I am suggesting that the inclusion of women in studies of managerial leadership might do more than suggest footnotes about this "special case." I am suggesting, rather, that the inclusion of women in the study of leadership might challenge and redefine basic assumptions about the way people in positions of authority behave.

For example, Slater (1955) studied role differentiation in small groups and provided evidence for the theory that two distinct types of leaders exist, task leaders and social-emotional leaders. In Slater's groups, emergent leaders played either the task-leader role or the social-emotional leader role. No one performed both of these functions for a group. Slater's subjects, notably, were all Harvard men. A preliminary study by the author (Heller, 1978) indicates that when women serve as leaders (in a group composed of both men and women) this division of labor does not exist. Each woman who leads performs both functions providing both task and social emotional leadership.

Kanter (1977) points out that one aspect of the dynamics of introducing a new type person into a homogeneous group is that the sameness of the original group is heightened. Similarly, the inclusion of women in the study of leadership at once points to the limits of the study of American men in hierarchical organizations and opens new vistas to exploration. I hope that this book will open some such vistas. Part One serves to underline the influence of organizational culture, traditions, ideologies, and values upon leaders. Part Two introduces the self-perceptions of leaders as well as the viewpoints of the leaders' peers and superiors—thus underlining the limits of the study of the leader-follower dyad. Part Three is an attempt to place the study of leadership in organizations into the broader context of American society —a society in the process of change.

Trudy Heller
Philadelphia, Pennsylvania

CHAPTER ONE: MYTHS

"Over the centuries femininity has been stereotyped as dependent, submissive and conforming, and hence women have been seen as lacking in leadership qualities . . . . . The male bias is reflected in the false conception of leadership as mere command or control. As leadership comes properly to be seen as a process of leaders engaging and mobilizing the human needs of followers, women will be more readily recognized as leaders and men will change their own leadership styles."

James MacGregor Burns, *Leadership*

Leadership has been studied since ancient times, but only recently have these studies included women, or looked at sex differences. The "great man" theory of leadership was one of the earliest. According to this theory, leaders were born into their role. Research focused on attempts to define the qualities or personality traits which were part of a leader's inheritance, distinguishing him from others, (Stogdill, 1974). As the name of the theory indicates, one of these traits was being a man.

Another of the earlier theories was the situational or environmental theory. According to this theory, leadership arose to meet the demands of the situation. The person who performed the leadership role was considered to be a mere instrument through which the needs of the situation were met. This theory ignored all qualities of the individuals in the leadership role, including gender.

Both of these one-sided theories, the traits theory and the situational theory, were proven through research to be inadequate, (Mann, 1959). More comprehensive theories developed which conceived of leadership as a product of the individual leader interacting with the environment. Fiedler's Contingency Theory and Homans' Exchange Theory are examples of interactive models of leadership.

As the interactive models of leadership developed, many of the major research studies still were conducted with all male samples and no awareness of sex effects. The classic Ohio State Leadership Studies, for example, used samples of Air Force flight crews, school superintendents, foremen in manufacturing plants, and ROTC cadets, (Stogdill and Coons, 1957). As late as 1974, Ralph Stogdill's comprehensive *Handbook of Leadership: Theory and Research* omits any reference to women or sex role in its index or contents.

Another source of the male bias in the conception of leadership comes from the development of management science which followed the growth of modern industry in the early part of the twentieth century. The major proponent of this new science was Frederick Winslow Taylor. He emphasized the need for rationality, logical thought and objectivity as managerial traits. These traits, of course, are all traditionally male, (Kanter, 1977a, p. 20-23).

In spite of the long-standing traditional male bias, several forces have served to promote the presence of women in leadership roles in recent years. The Women's Movement has awakened the desire of many women to seek the rewards of leadership. The new laws on equal employment opportunity have created the opportunity for some of them to do so. The development of the school of thought, Human Relations in Industry,[1] has introduced such "feminine" values as communication among co-workers and sensitivity to feelings of subordinates, complementing Taylor's model of the rational, male manager. Finally, the development of role theory and the introduction of the concept "sex role" has led to the study of sex effects in leadership.

This research has gone through three phases as the number of women in leadership roles has increased. In the earliest phase, studies demonstrated the under-representation of women in leadership ranks and addressed the need for more equal representation. Later studies focused on defining psychological and sociological barriers to women assuming leadership roles. The most recent research has focused on understanding the dynamics of leadership for women and men, exploring differences and similarities.

One of the most interesting topics, both among academic researchers and popular writers, is the phenomenon of sex role stereotyping. At the same time that female leaders are becoming increasingly commonplace, so is evidence of various negative stereotypes of women as leaders. These images can be found in the media every day. Rather than dissipating the stereotypes, the real presence of female leaders seems to have raised consciousness of these images and to have created a proliferation of varieties.

The cover story of *Ms Magazine* in September 1978, depicted four negative stereotypes of women who wield power over other women (Hammer, 1978). The first image was the "earth mother "—the office inhabitant who brings home-baked chocolate chip cookies to meetings, and keeps a communal bottle of aspirin in her desk which she doles out with the verbal equivalent of chicken soup. The second feminine power-wielder was the "manipulator" who relies on feminine wiles to get her way. The third image was of the "workaholic" whose weakness is the inability to delegate responsibility. Hence, she ends up doing it all herself. Finally, we have the image of the "egalitarian" leader who denies the power of her leadership role altogether, and claims to relate to subordinates as a colleague.

Another typology, which is based on more systematic research, appeared in *Psychology Today* in an article entitled "Why Bosses Turn Bitchy" by Rosabeth Moss Kanter, (1976). Dr. Kanter finds four stereotypes of lady bosses as they related to their predominantly male cohorts: "Mother" also appears in this typology. "Pet" is the little sister or mascot of the group. The "sex object" fails to establish herself as a professional. And the "iron maiden" tries too hard to establish herself as a professional and comes to be seen as more tyrannical than she intends to be or really is.

Both of these typologies place female leaders at one or the other extreme of a continuum. At one pole is the woman who is too submissive and/or emotional to be an effective leader, as the mother, pet, sex object, and egalitarian. At the other pole is the woman who is aggressive, domineering, the "bitchy" lady boss as personified by the iron maiden, workaholic, and manipulator. The omitted successful leaders presumably are in the middle ground: the person who can manage power but also knows how to delegate, can be decisive but can also listen to subordinates and be sensitive.

When real women who lead are depicted in the media, their features are frequently compared and contrasted to these composite images. Georgia Rosenbloom who inherited ownership of the Los Angeles Rams was featured in a cover story of the Sunday New York *Times Magazine,* (Kaiser, 1979). The tone of the article was one of surprise. This woman whose history as a showgirl evoked the images of the emotional, sexual and submissive female, was turning out to be a powerful, hardworking leader. Her strength was exemplified by the firing of her stepson as the Rams' manager shortly after assuming her position.

But the real surprise was that based on the bottom line, the performance record of the Rams, she was a successful leader. Her success was in spite of the fact that she evoked negative images of two extreme types of leaders: the frivolous sex object at one extreme and the domineering iron-maiden at the other. According to the author, both he and the entire sports world were dumbfounded by this phenomenal woman who was so unamenable to stereotyping.

While a variety of female images have developed, the singular image of the strong, aggressive, rational and aloof male leader has remained. When Mrs. John Connally is campaigning for her husband in the New Hampshire primaries, she stands up before the crowd (and the television audience) and declares that he is "strong" and "tough."[2]

ROLE THEORY

The media are not alone in reflecting an interest in male-female stereotypes. In the scholarly literature, too, a great deal of attention has been paid to the nature and function of sex-role stereotyping. Most of this research has focused on women, and has been couched in the theoretical framework of role theory.

In recent years role theory has gained recognition as one of the most productive viewpoints from which to research leadership phenomena.   Ralph Stogdill (1974, p. 15) states that "of all available definitions, the role conception of leadership is most firmly buttressed by research findings." Katz and Kahn (1966) cite the role concept as being "singularly promising" in understanding the entire field of individuals in social systems.

Role theory provides a model for the process of role definition. The process is a cycle of interaction between the leader or the "focal person" and various "role senders" who work with the leader as subordinates, peers or superiors, and who communicate to the leader their expectations of how s/he should behave. (Thomas and Biddle, 1966).

Katz and Kahn (1966) emphasize that the "expectations" of the role senders are not passive fantasies of how the leader should behave, but are forceful attempts to influence the leader. Role senders will provide rewards and sanctions appropriately as the leader conforms or fails to conform to their expectations.

At the other end of the cycle, the leader, receiving the expectations of the role senders, will react either by conforming to the expectations or not. The leader's behavior may also alter the expectations of the role senders, and the cycle begins again.

A study of school superintendents by Gross, McEachern and Mason (1975) demonstrated that these leaders were making judgements about whether the expectations they received for their role were "legitimate" or not.   When a superintendent perceived the expectation as being legitimate, he conformed his behavior to the expectation.   When the expectation was seen as being illegitimate, he did not conform.

The complexity of the leadership role and the process of role definition creates the possibility of role conflict and role ambiguity.   The importance of these phenomena have been borne out through studies in which the effects of role conflict and role ambiguity have almost always been shown to be detrimental to the leader in terms of job satisfaction and effectiveness in the organization.

The findings of Robert Kahn and his colleagues reveal the consequences of role conflict and role ambiguity as follows:

> . . . objective role conflict (measured by the statement of role senders that they wished for specific changes in the focal person's behavior) was related to low job satisfaction, and a high degree of job related tension. The effects of role ambiguity (defined as a lack of information regarding supervisory evaluation of one's work, about opportunities for advancement, scope of responsibility, and expectations of role senders) were in general comparable to those of role conflict. Persons subjected to conditions of ambiguity on the job tended to be low in job satisfaction, low in self-confidence, high in tension and a sense of futility, (Katz and Kahn, 1966, p. 190).

In the study of school superintendents by Gross, et al., (1975) it was shown that high job satisfaction was related to a superintendent and his school board holding similar definitions of the superintendent's role. When a superintendent had different expectations for himself than those of the board, he tended to have low job satisfaction.

Role conflict poses particular difficulties for female leaders. In the langauge of role theory, a woman who occupies a position of leadership is enacting both a sex role, woman, and an organizational role, leader. The former role is differentiated from the other by an act of birth, and the latter is differentiated by the set of behaviors which are expected of the person occupying such a position, (Thomas and Biddle, 1966).

Because of this dual role, women are vulnerable to role conflict. One kind of role conflict exists when the female leader's co-workers (subordinates, peers, superiors) have conflicting expectations of how a woman should behave and how a leader should behave. This conflict will be communicated to the leader, creating a lack of clarity as to how she is expected to behave in her leadership position, (Katz and Kahn, 1966).

Many studies of women in leadership roles focus on the attitudes or expectations of the leader's co-workers. Studies which look at sex role stereotyping, for example, are raising the question: Is there conflict between the expected behavior of a woman and the expected behavior of a manager? These studies provide evidence for and against the notion that a special kind of conflict exists for a woman in a position of leadership, i.e., a conflict between expectations for her as a woman, and expectations for her as a leader. However, more studies report evidence of such conflict than do not.

Another kind of role conflict which is peculiar to women leaders is the conflict arising from attitudes held by the leader herself. When a woman in a position of leadership has one set of expectations for herself as a woman and another conflicting set of expectations for herself as a leader, then she experiences conflict.

In the literature review of attitudinal barriers to women entering managerial positions, O'Leary (1974) finds such conflict. Studies are cited which indicate that even while performing leadership roles calling for self-confidence and high achievement, the women in these roles hold attitudes towards themselves as women which include low self-esteem, fear of failure, and expectations of negative consequences of engaging in achievement oriented behavior.

Another way in which women are theoretically vulnerable, according to the role theory conception of leadership, is in the achievement of "role legitimation." Role theory provides this term to describe the fact that however a leader acquires his/her position, the power and authority of the position must be recognized by followers, peers, and superiors. Although different leader behaviors lead to legitimation in different circumstances, a generalization is that "the extent to which the leader is able to fulfill these expectations [of followers, peers, superiors] tends to determine the degree to which groups concerned will legitimate the leadership role," (Stogdill, 1974, p. 323).

An assumption of the theory is that leadership does not come automatically with the job title, manager or principal. Although organizational lines of command may be backed by the rational-legal authority of the organization with leaders having powers to reward and punish subordinates, and although an organization may be seen as a system of interlocking roles, the persons in those roles determine to a large extent how they are enacted.

But what if the expected role is one of the diverse images of female leaders which is negatively valued? How then does the woman gain recognition or legitimation of her leadership position? Common sense declares that playing into one of these negatively valued roles, e.g., mother or sex object, will *not* lead to recognition of her authority. Yet the role theory model declares that fulfilling the expectations of followers, peers and superiors, (whatever these expectations may be) is the only way to achieve legitimation of the leadership role.

Obviously this particular dilemma would not exist for a man in a leadership position. Expecting him to behave like a man is synonymous with expecting him to be a good manager, i.e., strong, aggressive, and business-like.

Because the importance of stereotyping is so strongly underlined by the role theory conception of leadership, the following questions become very significant indeed: What are the contempoary images of women and men as leaders? On the path to leadership styles of the future (Chapter 8) from the traditional image of the male manager, how far have we come? Are we stuck with the male image as many studies of sex-role stereotyping lead us to believe? Is this such an unchangeable image that no matter how many Georgia Rosenblooms surprise us, we persist in equating maleness with managerial skill?

CONTEMPORARY STEREOTYPES

In order to assess the current reality, I conducted a comparative study of women and men in organizational leadership roles. The leaders in the study were six male-female pairs, matched on rank, job responsibilities and the kind of organization in which they worked. In addition to the leaders themselves, information was gathered from subordinates, peers and superiors. The ninety-one people who participated in the study represented a wide variety of different kinds of organizations.

The first pair of leaders were both directors of social service agencies whose client populations were prisoners. The two agencies were structurally similar; each director reported to a board of directors and was responsible for

supervising a staff of administrative assistants and counselors. The directors' peer groups consisted of heads of other
social service, law enforcement, and governmental agencies.

The second pair were both administrators in a large,
urban public school system. Both had offices in one of the
central administration buildings of the school system. The
two administrators were responsible for training and staff
development functions. Both supervised a staff of trainers
and a secretary who worked with personnel in a number of
different schools.

The third pair of leaders were managers in a small
business, a travel agency. They were the only employees at
the managerial level, and the superior to whom they reported
was the owner of the business. Each manager supervised a
staff of travel agents.

The fourth pair of leaders were both directors of alcoholism clinics which were part of a state mental health
system. Each clinic serviced a different geographic area, and
was located in the area it served. Each director reported to
an administrator of the state mental health system, and
supervised a staff of counselors and secretaries.

The fifth pair of leaders were project directors in the
same department of a large corporation. Their superior was
the director of the department. The department was structured as a matrix system, and subordinates were assigned to
the directors for specific projects.

The sixth pair of leaders were department heads in
universities. Both universities were located in urban settings
and both had similar student populations, i.e., first generation
to go to college. These leaders reported to the deans of the
colleges in which their departments were located. Their
subordinates were the faculty members and secretaries of the
departments.

In interviews with 65 of the men and women in these
organizations, two sets of images emerged: one set of negative stereotypes of the female and of the male leader, and
another set of positive images. When I asked men and women
to describe difficulties they had had with male and female
supervisors, what emerged was a set of negative images of
the male and of the female leader. In some respects, women
and men were decribed as erring in opposite directions.
Women were seen as being too emotional and demonstrative;
men were seen as being too remote and inaccessible. Other

weaknesses were attributed to both women and men, but in different amounts. Both men and women were criticized for being too authoritarian and aggressive; however, this quality was attributed to men more often than to women. In no case was the same negative quality ascribed to both women and men in the same way. Women and men were seen as leaders with distinctly different weaknesses. (See Figure 1.)

FIGURE 1

Contemporary Stereotypes of Women and Men as Leaders

Negative Images

1. too focused on procedures (men)	1. too focused on people (women)
2. remote, inaccessible (men)	2. emotionally demonstrative (women)
3. authoritarian, aggressive (men and women)	3. not assertive (women)
4. sexist (men)	

Positive Images

Women	Men
1. more humane	1. relaxed, humorous
2. open, friendly	2. separate work and social roles
3. egalitarian	3. think categorically
4. efficient and organized	4. work independently

FOCUS ON PROCEDURES VS. FOCUS ON PEOPLE

Men Are Too Focused on Procedures

Many people expressed a sort of regret at not having an easier rapport with their male bosses. The men were seen as imposing such narrow limits on their relationships with subordinates that working together was difficult. "We had a strained relationship because he would only discuss work," commented one worker about her supervisor. This regret was voiced by both women and men.

Another form that this complaint took was an unfulfilled desire for nurturance and support from a male supervisor. "He didn't understand my needs." "He wasn't appreciative of my work." "He couldn't forgive and forget." These comments echo the regret of having such a limited, all-business relationship with a male boss that even the basic emotional need for support of one's work was not gratified. One industrial worker commented: "[My boss] didn't appreciate how difficult a job can be. While I realize no one likes to hear excuses coming, I think there has to be an understanding of what it takes to get a job done and done right."

Other times the impersonality of a male boss was described as rudeness, inconsiderateness. A woman who was a trainer of teachers for a school system describes her anger at not being treated with greater sensitivity and understanding by her boss in this incident: "[I] received notice that they had to make room for me in another office, and [my boss] took me into his office and very abruptly said: '_____, you're moving to such and such a school.' Then I did something that I don't like to do and went over his head to ask someone above him if I could stay, and I did. Then I went back to him and told him that I'd been very upset that he had treated me that way, with sort of an insensitivity. I was pleased that I went through this process. I also felt good that I'd gotten support from the people above him. [The support] made me feel appreciated."

Finally, male supervisors' impersonality was described as undermining not just the emotional basis for work, i.e., rapport, support, recognition of one's needs, but as being directly destructive of the creative process of work. "He was inflexible and had rigid expectations." "He stifled my creativity." Refusing to accept suggestions for change was the complaint of this worker: "In the _____industry there are old ways . . . MBA's bring in new technologies. The old men don't want to change their thinking. [They] should listen. I feel that the biggest problem is that they don't want to change their thinking."

Women Are Too Focused on People

Often the female supervisor who personalized work issues was cast in a mother role. "She treated people who worked with her like children." "She pulled rank in a demeaning way." These comments came from people who were angry because they felt that they had personally been criticized when their work should have been the issue. A female worker descibed a boss who assigned work hours on a personal, unsystematic basis: "She [the boss] played favorites. It was a question of another woman and I wanting more hours. She [the other worker] knew how to play on this woman's sympathies, and got the hours."

Conflict situations were cited as being especially difficult for women to handle without getting too personal. One worker noted that men could go into a meeting, argue strongly for different sides of an issue, and come out shaking hands. Women, however, could not forgive and forget so easily after an argument.

One female director had personalized conflict between her agency and other agencies to such an extent that her staff described her as having an "us against the world" mentality. They felt great pressure to agree with the director one hundred percent or else be seen as disloyal, as one of "them," "the enemy."

The use of feminine wiles was also criticized as an illegitimate use of the personal mode in conflict situations. "She played on people's sympathies to get her way," was a comment that was made about a female director who did not fight fair.

EMOTIONALLY DEMONSTRATIVE VS. REMOTE, INACCESSIBLE

Women Are Too Emotional

One of the consequences of personalizing work issues is that women were criticized for being over-emotional. "She was easily excited, angered." "She was temperamental, moody." "She cried during meetings." Such displays of emotion made co-workers uncomfortable, and undermined the female leader's authority, as illustrated by the following description of an assistant school principal: "[She] got so emotional (excited, angry) that people stopped going to her, being afraid she would blow up."

Other workers criticized female supervisors for not knowing how to separate professional and social roles. Bringing personal problems to work was one complaint. Antoher was to focus on such traditionally feminine issues as interior decoration. Hence the following comment about a female school superintendent: "When I first came in the [school] system, the district superintendent, a woman, came in and commented that the shades were crooked."

Men Are Too Remote, Inaccessible

On the other hand, male supervisors were criticized for being too remote and inaccessible. Very different from the overly involved and personal mother hen, is the man who is "quiet and withdrawn from subordinates", "not even aware of what's going on." These commentators saw their male supervisors as having retiring personality traits which were incompatible with the managerial role. In one case, organizational policy was used as a protective shield: "Instead of dealing with issues, he would point to the policy or job description."

Other workers saw their male supervisors' remoteness as being more deliberate: "He kept information to himself." "He was not in when you called to keep an appointment." These workers are describing male supervisors who chose to distance themselves from subordinates as a way of retaining their power. "The type of individual who piecemeals a project so he's the only one with the big picture. Keeps things to himself. Doesn't want subordinates to know as much as he does." Or, a more extreme case: "One supervisor failed to provide the information necessary for the completion of a project."

agnesyum v mie stonowccy

AUTHORITARIAN, AGGRESSIVE VS. NOT ASSERTIVE

Both Women and Men Can Be Too Authoritarian

Both men and women were criticized for being too authoritarian or aggressive. But this complaint was directed to men more frequently than to women. Also, the focus of the complaints was different for men and for women.

For male leaders, the major form that this complaint took was that the men were too directive about how work should be done: "Decisions came down from the top to be carried out to the letter." "He was always looking over my shoulder, wanted things done *his* way." One secretary described her new boss: "When Mr. C. first came I had some difficulty adjusting to him after being secretary to the executive for sixteen years . . . I used to make my own decisions, and follow through on things. When Mr. C. came, he told me to do things which I felt I didn't need to be told because a secretary should know how to do them."

A similar complaint was that the men were too demanding in terms of how much work should be done: "He expected too much." "He created a tremendous amount of pressure." "He asked me to perform duties that were not part of the job, like picking up his girlfriend."

Another quality ascribed to the authoritarian male boss was an inability to accept ideas (especially critical ones) from subordinates: "He inhibited questioning of the structure." "He was defensive at criticism." These comments describe the frustrations of subordinates who attempted and failed to create a flow of communication from the bottom up rather than from the top down.

In one case, a female teacher's ideas were acceptable to her male principal only when he presented them as his own: "We [the teacher and her boss, the principal] would talk over a situation. He would say, 'What do you think?' If my opinion was to change something then maybe a month later he would take my suggestion to the faculty as if it were his own idea."

Sometimes the authoritarian male leader was described as being personally offensive. It was not just that he was picky about the way work was to be done, but he interacted with subordinates in a way that left them feeling intimidated, or demeaned. "He was like a father, treated me like a kid." "He was tyrannical, arrogant." "He came across as a tough character, was abusive and belittling." "He blew up at me all the time." "I had to crawl on my hands and knees to get along with him." The deep-seated humiliation described in these remarks is clearly not the best emotional climate for productive work. A mental health worker describes the disruption of her work: "Once he [my boss] gave me the dickens over lost keys when he did the same thing [lost keys]. He used to blow up at me all the time, but if it got too bad, and he cursed and screamed, I would just leave and walk down to the ladies' room."

When female leaders were described as being too authoritarian, however, the comments did not _reveal_ the feelings of the subordinates. Instead, the comments focused on a sort of disdain or negative judgment of the female leader. "She was dictatorial, treated the workers like children." She was "bossy," "bitchy," "domineering," "stubborn," "intolerant." The vast majority of comments about authoritarian female leaders were judgments of the leader's personality.

A few of the comments concerned the female leader's work style as being either too interfering, e.g., "She was too concerned about little things, too critical," or too ambitious, e.g., "She let herself be known as THE LEADER when it wasn't necessary." "She would kill to get ahead."

Women Are Not Assertive Enough

Only women were described as lacking assertiveness. Sometimes comments were very direct in this criticism: "She was not willing to direct others to the extent required." "She passed the buck rather than dealing with issues herself."

In one case, a female leader was described as being pretty, and therefore, having the particular problem of good looking women, i.e., not being taken seriously. This woman was seen as lacking the extra amount of assertiveness that would have been required to overcome the handicap of being an attractive woman.

Men Are Sexist

Only one commentator described a female boss as being sexist. "She was a sexist and went out of her way to put men down." This comment articulates the fear of men that a female boss may be one of those "libbers" who is angry at all men.

Otherwise, remarks about sexism were directed to male leaders. Some remarks described direct sexual overtures: "He expected the female staff to sleep with him." "He wanted to have sex with me." Other comments were on less direct forms of sexism. "He wouldn't acknowledge accomplishments from a woman." "I took advantage of being a woman occasionally to get around specific work requirements by being coy, bright, charming." These female subordinates are saying that their work was treated unfairly (either too harshly or too easily) because they were females working for a male boss.

POSITIVE STEREOTYPES

I also asked people to describe differences in the ways that women and men work. What came out of the responses to this question is the notion that both women and men have special resources that they bring to the workplace. Whether these differences are the result of inherent male-female differences or differences in upbringing and experience does not matter. The point is that in the present state of society, women and men have different strengths as workers and as leaders.

Women Are More Humane

Women were described, first of all, as being more humane than men. This is the positive side of personalizing issues at work. Women are able to sense and understand the personal motives and interests of their workers, and are more willing to bend the rules to accommodate emotional needs. They are sensitive to the human processes of turning out work, and do not focus solely on the product. A division chief in a large industrial organization who had female project directors working for him summed up this quality in a comment: "I think women tend to have a human orientation more than men. They tend to look at people as people rather than someone who turns out work."

How is this humanity demonstrated? Sometimes, it's in the tone of voice and phrasing of a request for work. A male industrial worker who had just completed work on a project that was directed by a woman commented "Women may go at things on a more personal basis. A man might say, 'This is what's to be done,' whereas a woman may say, 'This is what I have to do, how can you help me?'"

Another man who had worked on the same project also remarked about the difference in conversational tone: "Women definitely take a more peronal touch to their work. You'll find that you talk on a more personal level than with men, more open, more friendly. They [women] would make good salesmen."

Hence, another way in which feminine humanity is demonstrated is through the presentation of an open and friendly manner. Women engage their workers in conversation more often, and are seen as being more open to feedback from subordinates. They try harder to accept and understand their workers, and therefore are "slower to come to the boiling point."

Women Are Egalitarian

Finally, female workers demonstrate their humanity by running the office according to egalitarian principles. Everyone is treated more like a peer or a colleague, and less like a subordinate or inferior. Hence the flow of communication between female leaders and subordinates goes in both directions. An office worker in a social service agency that was directed by a woman described her workplace: "Looking at this office, there's less rank. If the phone rings, anyone will pick up the phone. People make their own calls. There's more warmth and conversation, less status things. For instance, one woman here became pregnant and everyone in the office knew before her husband. And it was the accountant (a man) who told him when he came in at noon."

Women Are Efficient and Organized

In addition to being more humane, women are seen as having special resources in organization and efficiency. Women are seen as being attentive to detail. "They are sticklers for neatness and punctuality." "They are more efficient." In appropriate amounts, and places, these are highly valued organizational skills.

Men Are Relaxed, Humorous

Male leaders were complimented on having a sense of humor. The male leader is typically more sure of himself in his leadership role. This confidence is reflected in a relaxed and humorous manner.

Another way in which male leaders express their confidence is by speaking directly. "Men come more directly to the point." An important aspect of the male leader's strength is an ability to breach sensitive issues in a forthright manner.

Men Separate Work and Social Roles

Men are also more sure about the boundaries between work and social roles. "Men reserve socializing for after hours." Their humorous and relaxed manner in the office extends only to business matters. They are pros at being business-like and do not bring personal issues to the workplace.

Men can maintain the separation of work and social roles even in a conflict situation. A female school administrator made the following observation of her male colleagues: "I think men can swear at each other in a meeting and go out of there with their arms around each other. Women [on the other hand] get emotional about things."

Men Think Categorically, Work Independently

Two elements are part of the male leader's business sense: (1) the ability to think categorically, and (2) a capacity for working independently. Categorical thinking enables men to see broader organizational issues rather than getting caught up in detail or in personalities. An independent work style enables men to stick to business without taking time out to seek support and socialize.

Has anything changed? There certainly is nothing new about the notion that women are better at the human side of enterprise, more emotional, more sensitive to feelings. Nor is there anything different about the notion that men are more task oriented, better able to think categorically as well as more aggressive and competitive than women. The stereotypes of the strong, aggressive and aloof male, and of the soft, emotional female are old themes that are familiar to everyone. *pousciaglivey*

In 1972, Inge Broverman and colleagues published a comprehensive study of sex-role stereotypes. After developing a questionnaire and administering the instrument to approximately 1,000 people in various walks of life, the researchers concluded:

> "Our research demonstrates the contemporary existence of clearly defined sex-role stereotypes for men and women . . . Women are perceived as relatively less competent, less independent, less objective and less logical than men; men are perceived as lacking interpersonal sensitivity, warmth and expressiveness in comparison to women." (Broverman, et. al., 1972, p. 75).

Taking a closer look at the specific characteristics that Broverman's subjects found to be typically masculine or typically feminine, there is a great deal of overlap with the typologies of women and men as leaders described above. Concerning the negative images, Broverman's "average men" were described as being "very aggressive" and "very dominant" (authoritarian, aggressive).   Men were also described as "not at all emotional" and "not at all easily influenced" (remote, inaccessible). Concurring with the positive side, Broverman's "average man" was described as being "very logical" (thinks categorically), "very direct" (separates work and social roles), and "very self-confident" (relaxed, humorous).

Concurring with the positive image of the female leader, Broverman's subjects noted the "average woman" as being "very aware of feelings of others" (more humane), and "very neat in habits" (efficient, organized).

The negative images of the female leader, however, were the most thoroughly substantiated by Broverman's checklist. As for women being too focused on people, Broverman's subjects described women as "not at all independent," "very subjective," "not at all skilled in business," "does not know the ways of the world." Concurring with the image of women as too emotionally demonstrative, Broverman's subjects said women are "very emotional," "very excitable in a minor crisis," "feelings easily hurt," "cries very easily" and "unable to separate feelings from ideas." And concurring with the image of women being non-assertive, Broverman's subjects described women as "not at all aggressive," "very submissive," "not at all competitive," "almost never acts like a leader," "not at all ambitious."

A few years after Broverman's study, Virginia Schein (1973) conducted a study of sex role stereotypes with a context more specifically related to leadership. In "The Relationship Between Sex Role Stereotypes and Requisite Management Characteristics," she reports on a poll of male managers. Schein (1975) repeated the study with a sample of female managers. Again, the results concur with the female-male images presented above.

Concurring with negative images, Schein's managers more similar to men than to women were described as having "no desire for friendship" (too focused on procedures, remote and inaccessible), as being "competitive," "aggressive," "forecful," "ambitious" (authoritarian, aggressive).

Concurring with the positive images, men were described as self-confident, emotionally stable, steady (relaxed, humorous); as objective, consistent (separates work and social roles); as logical, having analytic ability (thinks categorically).

Validating the positive images of female leaders, Schein's managers more similar to women than men were described as being more humane in terms of having "humanitarian values," being "aware of feelings of others," being "helpful," "cheerful," and "intuitive."

Finally, the images of female and male leaders of this study concur with Kanter's (1976) typology of female leaders. Kanter's "mother" is too focused on people and too emotionally demonstrative. Her "pet" is non-assertive. The sex object has all three failings: She is too focused on people, too emotional, and not assertive enough. The "iron maiden" is too emotional with a negative charge (it is her hostile emotions that people fear), and she may also be sexist.

The content of the images of males and females that emerges from these studies is so consistent that it tends to either confirm the existence of biological differences or point to the notion that the women's movement is in a very early phase indeed! Perhaps this issue will only be resolved with the passage of time. Will these images be the same in ten years time?

But to dwell on this point evades two questions which are more important for understanding the impact of sex role stereotypes on women and men who lead. The first question is: How do stereotypes *operate* in the day-to-day activities of the workplace? The second question is: How are the characteristically male or female qualities, strengths or weakness, valued by subordinates, peers and superiors? Is there change occurring in the value placed on "sensitivity to feelings," for example, if not on its attribution as a feminine trait?

These are the questions that will be addressed in the remainder of this book. Chapters two, three and four will address the question of how stereotyped images of male and female leaders function in the work lives of individual women and men who lead. Chapters five and six describe the images that male and female leaders hold of themselves. Chapter seven explores nuances in the imaging process for people in different power relationships to the leader. Finally, chapter eight assesses these contemporary data in terms of what they indicate about future trends. Has anything changed? What are the prospects for change continuing and in what directions? Are any of the changes being given permanence through incorporation into organization structures and policies?

NOTES

1. The beginning of the interest in industrial workers as human beings that relate to one another in the workplace is commonly attributed to Elton Mayo and his well-known Hawthorne studies.
2. The statement by Mrs. Connaly was aired in a taped segment on the CBS Evening News in February, 1980.

CHAPTER TWO: WOMEN AND MEN WHO LEAD— BUSINESS ORGANIZATIONS

> "Because work is the main proving ground of masculinity, all the 'male' traits, not just competitiveness, must be displayed there. Toughness is valued, often as an end in itself, without real consideration of whether or not it is in fact functional."

Marc Feigen Fasteau, *The Male Machine*

> "Such token male roles as achievers and bosses may represent counterparts to female roles as mascot, seductress, iron maiden and mother."

Carol Tropp Schreiber, *Changing Places: Men and Women in Transitional Occupations*

Eileen Grant,[1] manager of retail sales, was going through a divorce. She occasionally left her office in a small suburban business for two or three hours at a time, either at the lunch hour or later in the afternoon. During these absences, she did not let the people who worked for her know where she was going.

Eileen was severely criticized for this behavior both by the people she supervised and by other employees in the small organization. In many other ways she was considered to be competent, but there was general agreement in her office that in taking leave unannounced she was not being a good manager.

In terms of role theory, Eileen could be described as playing a dual role in her organization: the role of a woman and the role of a manager. In many ways playing both of these roles at once presented no problem. She was basically viewed by co-workers as being a woman who was a good manager.

In the critical incidents of absence from the office, however, co-workers had different and conflicting beliefs about how a woman is likely to behave and how a good manager should behave. Women stereotypically lack the commitment to their work that managerial positions require.

Several factors have conributed to this image. Young women have tended to underestimate the number of years that they will participate in the labor force, and therefore have invested less than their male counterparts in education and training. Mothers have often dropped out of the job market during childbearing years. Wives have often been expected to relocate when and wherever their husbands' careers may dictate. Women have been concentrated in low-paid jobs where the turnover rate is high among both sexes. Finally, employers have selected women less often than men for training programs which would lead to job advancement and increased commitment to work (Barrett, 1979).

Although recent studies indicate that these trends are changing, the myth of the uncommitted female worker remains (Barrett, 1979). In the case of Eileen Grant, her behavior may have been so severely criticized because co-workers expected her to behave in accord with the stereotype of the woman as unstable worker. When she left the office without explanation repeatedly they had the evidence they needed to say: "See, a woman lacks the commitment to her work that is necessary to be a good manager." (No one mentioned that she produced less work or work of lower quality because of her absences.)

Had a male manager behaved the same way, his behavior may have simply been dismissed: "It's his prerogative as the boss." "It doesn't matter as long as he gets his work done well." His actions would be interpreted differently because the stereotypes of the male worker are quite different from those of the female worker. The male worker is very serious about his work, strives for positions of responsibility, and never lets home responsibilities interfere with his career. A greater number of absences would have been required before co-workers would begin to question their beliefs about the commitment of a man to his work.

In *The Male Machine*, Marc Feigen Fasteau (1974, p.135-136) describes a typical work day for the men of a New York law firm:

> "...associates would come in between nine and nine-thirty, drink coffee and read the paper until ten, take an hour and a half for lunch, play squash for an hour during the afternoon once or twice a week, at six-thirty go out for a drink and dinner at the client's expense, come back to the office about eight and work until ten or eleven. The same amount of work could have been done during a normal working day but that would not have demonstrated the same dedication to the firm required for promotion."

These men could easily have visited the divorce lawyer during lunch, squash or dinner breaks or before work without co-workers becoming disturbed.

Eileen Grant is one of four leaders from two business organizations who participated in the leadership study. These two male-female pairs of leaders represent the organizations where attitudes toward women as leaders are the *least* positive. Of the nine organizations represented in the study, the large industrial corporation ranked ninth and the small business ranked eighth on a measure of attitudes toward women as leaders.[2] Hence these four leaders are functioning in the most traditional climate of attitudes toward women— and therefore of men too.

Coincidental with the relatively negative attitudes toward women as leaders are strong traditions of male leadership in these organizations. An informant from the small business reports that it is traditionally a "women's business" with male owners. In other words, employees have been predominantly female or at least low paid—a sign of "women's work." The owners and profit takers of the businesses, however, have been predominantly male. An informant from the large corporation reports that his organization even employed male secretaries and clerical workers until about ten years ago.

The association of these two pieces of information: 1) the attitudes toward women as managers is the least positive in these two organizations, and 2) the presence of women in positions of leadership is the more recent, indicates that familiarity breeds acceptance of female leadership. How, then, do these four leaders fare in this climate?

A systematic description of these leaders as they are viewed by their subordinates, peers and superiors follows. Each leader is described in terms of a leadership style profile,[3] demographic characteristics of themselves and their work groups, co-workers' comments on the leader's strengths and weaknesses, and scores on two subscales of a standardized leader behavior questionnaire.[4]

SMALL BUSINESS

Eileen Grant and Dan Monroe are the only two managers of a small business. The owner of the business is their boss. The business is departmentalized by type of customer with Eileen in charge of commercial sales and Dan in charge of retail sales. Each of the two managers supervises a staff of sales personnel.

The leadership style profiles for Eileen Grant and her fellow manager, Dan Monroe, are presented in Figure 2-1. Each profile consists of eight categories organized around two dimensions: dominance-submission and hostility-affiliation. Each category is a combination of these dimensions, e.g., competitiveness is seen as a combination of dominance and hostility.

These dimensions relate well to the literature on sex-role stereotypes. In Kanter's (1976) typology, for example, the "mother" could be seen as dominant and affiliative, "iron maiden" as dominant and hostile, "sex object" and "pet" as submissive and affiliative. The male stereotype could be seen as more dominant and less affiliative than female counterparts.

A brief comparison of the profiles for Managers Monroe and Grant seems to indicate quite easily which of the pair is the woman and which is the man. Manager Monroe is much

FIGURE 2-1

Small Business

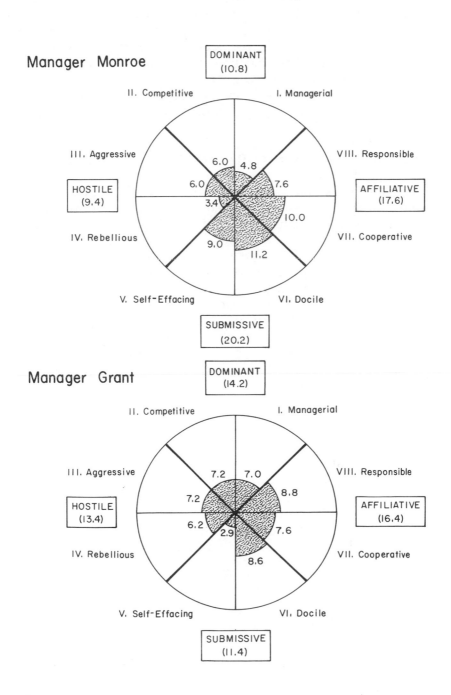

Manager Monroe

DOMINANT (10.8)

II. Competitive

I. Managerial

III. Aggressive

VIII. Responsible

HOSTILE (9.4)

AFFILIATIVE (17.6)

6.0 4.8
6.0 7.6
3.4
10.0
9.0
11.2

IV. Rebellious

VII. Cooperative

V. Self-Effacing

VI. Docile

SUBMISSIVE (20.2)

Manager Grant

DOMINANT (14.2)

II. Competitive

I. Managerial

III. Aggressive

VIII. Responsible

HOSTILE (13.4)

AFFILIATIVE (16.4)

7.2 7.0
7.2 8.8
6.2
2.9 7.6
8.6

IV. Rebellious

VII. Cooperative

V. Self-Effacing

VI. Docile

SUBMISSIVE (11.4)

more submissive and slightly more affiliative than Manager Grant. Manager Grant, on the other hand, is more dominant and more hostile than Manager Monroe. The stereotypes of the submissive, affiliative woman and the dominant male would clearly lead to the conclusion that Manager Monroe is a woman and Manager Grant is a man. The truth, however, is the opposite. A closer look at these leaders is required to make sense of this paradox, and to understand the impact of sex-role stereotypes on them.

Dan Monroe, Manager of Retail Sales

Dan Monroe is fifty-four years old and white. He completed some college work, but did not graduate. He has worked as the manager of retail sales of a suburban business for the past seven years, since its establishment. Dan expects this to be the job from which he will retire. He is remarried to a woman who does not work outside the home. Dan and his wife have three children.

Dan is older than his co-workers who range in age from twenty-seven to forty-four years, with an average age of thirty-six. He has as much or more seniority than his co-workers who have worked from one to seven years in the organization, with an average of four years of service. Dan's co-workers represent a variety of lifestyles in terms of marital status, number of hours that spouse works outside the home (if married) and number of children. His work group is balanced in terms of sex, consisting of three women and two men. No racial issues were reported (only one co-worker is black). Although three of Dan's co-workers (his boss, his fellow manager, and one subordinate) are college graduates and he is not, educational differences are not reported to be an issue for Dan in his leadership role. In sum, there is nothing remarkable about the demographic characterisitics of Dan Monroe's work group, nothing that would explain the extremely a-stereotypical profile that represents his style.

Co-workers' descriptions of Dan's strengths and weaknesses as a leader are, however, more enlightening. From his boss' point of view, Dan Monroe's strength is that he is honest and loyal. Furthermore, since his boss, the owner of the business, likes to rule with an iron hand himself, his comment about Dan is that "A great leader wouldn't work for me." In other words, Dan's submissiveness is compatible with his boss's expectation that the owner of the business be clearly viewed as the big boss.

The owner, on the other hand, sees Dan's "insecurity" and "lack of initiative" as a weakness in his manager's leadership style. He maintains that Manager Monroe is even "afraid of his employees."

Dan's relationship with his boss is oberved by his subordinates and cited as a sign of weakness: "He's afraid to approach the owner about things he would like to see." "He accepts the boss's word." "He doesn't stand up to the boss [because] he has made decisions in the past and been chopped down."

Other criticisms about Dan's submissiveness were not specific to his relationship with his boss, but were more general: "He's not a strong leader." "He does not fight." "He needs more backbone."

One critical incident which seemed to symbolize Dan's weakness as a leader was described by one of his subordinates: She went to Dan and requested that he speak to the owner about a pay raise for herself. She waited for what she believed was an appropriate amount of time. When the requested meeting between Manager Monroe and the owner had not yet taken place, the employee went around Dan and spoke up to the owner herself. In the end, she was granted the pay raise, and has never forgotten or forgiven Dan for his lack of initiative in this instance. She feels that he let her down.

On the positive side, the affiliative elements of Dan's style are appreciated. He is described by his subordinates as being a "nice guy," "easy to work for." This characteristic is not excessive, however. True to his male stereotype, Manager Monroe knows how to separate work and social roles. He can be "strictly business."

The lack of dominance and authoritarianism in Dan's style also fosters a relaxed work environment, which is conducive to creative work. One subordinate was pleased that he "allowed her to make her own decisions as long as it didn't hurt anyone." He was also complimented on being "not too strict" and "not too demanding."

These comments were borne out in Dan's scores on the Role Assumption Subscale of the Leader Behavior Description Questionnaire. (Role Assumption is defined as "actively exercises the leadership role rather than surrendering leadership to others.") Scores of individual co-workers were averaged for each item giving a composite view of the leader.

Dan's lowest scores were received on item #4) "He (never) lets some members take advantage of him." and item #6) "He (never) backs down when he ought to stand firm." The next lowest items were #1) "He is (never) hesitant about taking initiative in the group;" #2) "He (never) fails to take necessary action;" and #9) "He overcomes attempts to challenge his leadership." These lowest items concur with the reported weaknesses of Manager Monroe concerning his failure to stand up to his own boss, the owner of the business.

Dan's scores on the Initiation of Structure Subscale further validate co-workers comments. (Initiation of Structure is defined as "clearly defines own role and lets followers know what is expected of them.") The items of this subscale on which Dan received the lowest scores are #4) "He makes his attitudes clear to the group"; and #6) "He assigns group members to particular tasks." The next lowest item is #9) "He maintains definite standards of performance." The relatively low scores on these items underline Manager Monroe's reported weakness of lacking initiative.

One final point which can be drawn from the Initiation of Structure Subscale is that the highest items' point to Dan Monroe's conformity to his boss' directives: #2) "He encourages the use of uniform procedures;" #8) "He schedules work to be done;" and #10) "He asks that group members follow standard rules and regulations."

Eileen Grant, Manager of Commercial Sales

Eileen Grant is the manager of commercial sales in the same travel agency. She is a thirty-five year old black woman. She is a college graduate and has worked for the business for the past six years. She is separated from her husband, and has no children.

Eileen's co-workers range in age from twenty-two to forty-four years, with an average age older than herself, thirty-eight. One of her subordinates is a woman while the rest of her co-workers are men. All are white. The range of seniority of her subordinates is from one to three years in the organization. Eileen's subordinates are slightly less educated than the subordinates of her fellow manager, Dan Monroe, although she is a college graduate and Dan is not. (All of her subordinates who participated in the study have a high school education or less.) Eileen's co-workers represent a variety of lifestyles in terms of marital and family status.

This review of the demographic characteristics of Eileen Grant's co-workers leaves the impression that she is not working under very favorable circumstances. She is the only black employee in the group. She has one female subordinate, but her co-workers are largely male. She has a college degree that her fellow manager, her male peer, does not have. Her co-workers are, on the average, older than herself. One of her supervisees is thirteen years her senior.

In spite of these circumstances, Eileen Grant is generally viewed by co-workers as a competent leader. Her boss describes her as a "strong leader" who "controls" and "rules" the people she employs. She is able to stand up to challenges to her leadership. In his view, Eileen can "take heat." Her boss also admires her ambition. Her desire to advance is seen as a plus because it means that she works hard and is not afraid to take risks.

These strengths are echoed in the comments of her co-workers. Her ability to rule and control does not come across to subordinates as iron handed or excessive. To them, Eileen appears "decisive," "quick," "[ready to] step in and pick up the ball if there is a problem," "willing to explore problems in depth," and "[to have the] strength of her conviction."

Co-workers also perceive the ambition of Eileen Grant. They note that she "gives more than one hundred percent as a leader and as an employee." Her ambition is not the extreme of workaholism, however. Manager Grant simply "likes what she does."

One of the reasons her leadership may be so well legitimated as that she has the power base of expertise. She is cited by subordinates as "knowing her job." Her fellow manager sums up this view of her leadership very simply: "She knows what's to be done, and lets her people know what's to be done."

Another reason why this strong leader is so well accepted or legitimated is that subordinates see a considerate side of their boss: "She is able to get along with people." "She can talk with anyone." "She is pleasant." But her sensitivity is not so immoderate as to become excessive emotionality. This leader "does not get ruffled." She is just business-like enough.

Eileen's co-workers were nearly unanimous in describing her major weakness as a leader: "Her personal life can affect her job." The way in which it affected her job was that she was "not always at work," "would take two or three or four hour lunch breaks." To some co-workers this behavior was setting a bad example. To others, the absences made her dependability questionable.

Like her male counterpart, Dan Monroe, Eileen too was criticized because "she won't stand up to higher authority," i.e., the owner of the business. This criticism was much less universally voiced in relation to Eileen than in relation to Dan, however. Her relationship with her authoritarian boss may help to explain the lowest scored item on Eileen's Role Assumption Subscale (#4): "She lets some members take advantage of her."

Eileen's overall score on the Role Assumption Subscale was, however, considerably higher than the overall score of Dan Monroe (Eileen Grant: $\bar{X}$ = 4.2; Dan Monroe: $\bar{X}$ = 3.6). Dan Monroe received the lowest score on this scale of the twelve leaders included in the study.

On the Initiation of Structure Subscale, Eileen's overall score (4.16) was close to the score that Dan received (4.18). Some individual items, however, were scored differently in a way which helps to explain the two managers' style differences. Manager Grant's superior interpersonal relations with her staff is evident in the scoring of item #4: "He/she makes his/her attitudes clear to the group." While this was Eileen's highest item, it was Dan's lowest.

A difference in style is also brought out in the scoring of items #8 and #10: "He/she schedules work to be done." "He/she asks that group members follow standard rules and regulations." These are two of Eileen's lowest items and two of Dan's highest items. Eileen appears to be less rule-bound with her employees than Dan, her male counterpart.

LARGE INDUSTRIAL CORPORATION

Jim Stevens and Carol Victor are project directors in a large industrial corporation. Their boss is the director of their department. The department is structured as a matrix organization. For Jim and Carol this organizational design means that they are assigned to a project and given a staff of workers to supervise for the duration of the project. At the completion of the project, they are assigned to a new project and a new staff. Theoretically, the advantage of the matrix organization is that it allows the company to optimize the use of its human resources (Galbraith, 1973, p. 103-106).

The style profiles of Project Directors Stevens and Victor are presented in Figure 2-2. Examination of the profiles reveals that the two profiles are not very different. Director Stevens' profile is slightly more dominant and less affiliative than the profile of Director Victor. The major difference is in the hostility score where Director Stevens' score is more than twice the score of Director Victor.

In response to the questions, "Which leader is the man?" "Which is the women?", sex-role stereotypes do lead to the correct answer. The stereotypically more dominant and less affiliative Director Stevens is the male leader.

Jim Stevens, Project Director

Jim Stevens is thirty-seven years old and white. He has worked for the organization in which he is currently employed for seventeen years. His educational background includes a master's degree. He is married and has four children. His wife works outside the home part-time, less than twenty hours per week.

All of Jim's co-workers that were included in the study are white and male. All are either married or remarried. The majority of wives work outside the home at least part-time. The two wives who do not work have two children each.

Jim's subordinates range in age from thirty-one to thirty-four. Seniority of subordinates ranges from two to thirteen years. Educational background of the group includes one master's degree and two college graduates.

Jim's boss, the department head, is younger and has less seniority than Jim. The boss is thirty-four years old. He has just two years of experience in the organization.

In terms of these demographic characteristics, Director Stevens appears to be leading under favorable circumstances. He and his co-workers form a homogeneous group in terms of sex, race and marital status. His subordinates are younger, less senior and generally less educated than himself. The one

FIGURE 2-2

Large Industrial Corporation

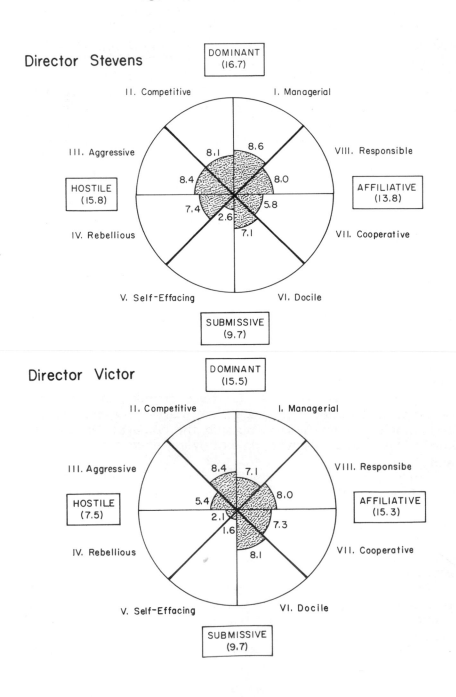

irregularity in Jim's situation is that his boss is younger and less senior than himself.

Jim's strengths as a leader rest partly upon his seniority and the expertise that he has developed over the years. His boss states that "he knows the [business] exceedingly well." Co-workers describe him as having "a lot of practical experience," as being "very knowledgeable in his field." "He puts out quality work."

His co-workers especially appreciate the fact that he has "come up the hard way." One consequence of this seniority is that he "understands many facets of the business." Another consequence is that he is "not afraid to get his hands dirty." "He leads by example when it's required." His supervision of subordinates is seen as being "helpful." Another consequence is that he is well connected in his organization. "He has contacts in every department; key men that he can go to."

Another strength related to his seniority is that he is seen as having the initiative to get into a new aspect of the business and learn the ropes: He has "a tremendous ability to get into a project that he knows very little about and get to know the details very well." His boss expresses confidence that he "can carry things through without being told what to do."

His other strengths as a leader cluster around his interpersonal abilities. He is described by co-workers as being "an extremely decent human being," "very honest, sincere." He can listen to his subordinates: "He is always open to new ideas; doesn't always follow the organized method. If it sounds good, he'll try it." He can also communicate with his subordinates: "He attempts to inform people he's working with."

In his supervision of subordinates, Jim is viewed as someone who can foster creativity and growth. "He's good at developing his people." He sets high standards and is demanding, but he also knows how to be helpful and how to support and guide his employees to achieve these high goals.

He is so good at developing his people that he sometimes loses them to other projects. Although the matrix organization in which Jim works is designed for personnel to rotate from project to project, the loss of staff is still viewed as a weakness: "One weakness may be related to the organization. He does not have a whole lot of control over staff. They get pulled out for other things."

Director Stevens' high standards (for himself and his employees) are also the key to another weakness as a leader. Sometimes his involvement in his work is too intense: "He tends to become personally involved in his project to the point where he's emotionally ego-involved in his work." One consequence of this intense involvement can be a failure to act: "He tends to be overcautious." "He over-checks before offering an opinion." Other times his subordinates bear the brunt of his perfectionism: "He can become terribly hard on the people who work for him as far as not giving them much leeway." This description would seem to explain the relatively high hostility score on Jim's style profile.

Jim's score on the Role Assumption Subscale is relatively low. Of all the twelve leaders in the study, his was the second lowest score. The two lowest items were: #4) "He (never) lets some members take advantage of him"; and #9) "He overcomes attempts to challenge his leadership."

These scores may partially be explained by the staffing situation of the matrix organization. The loss of staff may be seen as a challenge to his leadership. Another part of the explanation may lie in Jim's "niceness" and the way that quality differs from the tough male stereotype. Hence it may be viewed as a less strong form of leadership (measured by this traditional instrument of leader behavior).

Similarly, on the Initiation of Structure Subscale, Jim's score is relatively low. The highest items on this scale point to his expressiveness and ability to communicate with his staff: #1) "He lets group members know what is expected of them;" #4 "He makes his attitude clear to the group;" and #7) "He makes sure that his part in the group is understood by group members." The lowest items underline Jim's flexibility and willingness to bend the rules: #10) "He asks that members follow standard rules and regulations;" #8) "He schedules the work to be done;" and #2) "He encourages the use of uniform procedures".

Carol Victor, Project Director

Carol Victor is twenty-four years old and white. She is married and has no children. Her husband is a full-time student.

In sharp contrast to Jim Stevens' seniority, Carol has been in the company for just one year. The job in which she is currently employed is her first position after having received an MBA. Because the hiring and promotion of women is so new in this organization, however, this pair of leaders may be considered a typical case.

Carol's co-workers are also relatively young and inexperienced. Ages range from twenty-four to thirty-four with an average of twenty-seven. Seniority ranges from one to three years in the organization.

In terms of lifestyles, Carol's co-workers also have the characteristics of a young group. Of the two women and five men who participated in the study of Director Victor, two of the men have never been married. (The rest of the people are either married or remarried.) With the exception of her boss, none of Carol's co-workers has children. In addition to Carol's husband, one other spouse is a full-time student. The remaining spouses work outside the home more than twenty hours per week.

Compared to Jim Stevens' group, Carol's work group is more highly educated. All of her co-workers, except one, have master's degrees. The one exception is a law student.

Therefore, although Carol is younger and less experienced than her male counterpart, she is working under rather favorable conditions. In terms of maximizing her chances for success as a leader, her co-workers are well chosen. She is in a group which is similar in age, experience, and which is not all male—although the men remain in the majority.

One strength as a leader that was mentioned by several of her co-workers is Carol's intelligence: "She's very keen," "She's bright," "She has a fantastic memory."

Along with her capacity for doing the work, she has an enthusiasm for the job: She was described as "conscientious," "hard-working," "interested in getting into new areas," "sort of a doer."

In addition, Carol has organizational skills: "She appears to operate with direction and be organized." "She gets to the objective pretty quickly without getting waylaid by other details." "She uses discretion in her judgments."

The strength which is most unanimously talked about by her co-workers, however, concerns Carol's interpersonal abilities. As one co-worker worded it: "Her strengths are immediately obvious: she has relationships with people she needs to have relationships with." A somewhat more explicit version of this comment comes from another co-worker: "She comes across very easily and has no problems, no social barriers that other people may have." The most explicit version of this comment comes from yet another co-worker: "She doesn't seem to differentiate or is not inhibited by sex-role stereotypes. She manages very well to deal with situtions that come up." What these commentators seem to be saying is that for a young, attractive woman (she reports a history of sexual harassment on previous jobs) working in a man's world, she deals with the interpersonal aspects of her job remarkably well.

Still, her boss describes her weakness as being in "communication skills." He states that "she sometimes doesn't keep people informed of her output, of her results." He thinks that she does not communicate enough. (One cannot help but wonder if her failure to communicate on occasion is related to those "situations that come up" which were referred to in her co-workers' previous comments.)

The weakness that her co-workers describe relates to her image as bright, ambitious and hard-working. One co-worker comments, "She's so good that when she finds something she can't do she gets a little frustrated." Another comment also describes her tendency to get ahead of herself: "She might try to teach something over her head before investigating the situation."

Carol's composite score on the Role Assumption Subscale was the highest of the twelve leaders in the study ($\overline{X} = 4.53$). This score is in sharp contrast to her male counterpart, Jim Stevens, who ranked eleventh. Her highest items were #10) "She is easily recognized as the leader of the group;" #5) "She is (never) the leader of the group only;" and #7) "She is (never) hesitant about taking initiative in the group." These items echo her co-workers' comments concerning the legitimation or recognition of her authority as a leader.

Although her composite score on the Initiation of Structure Subscale is higher than the composite score of Jim Stevens, the highest and lowest items are identical. The lowest items concern rules and regulations: #10) "He/she asks that group members follow standard rules and regulations;" and #2) "He/she encourages the use of uniform procedures."

The highest items concern the structuring of work on a more individualized basis: #1) "He/she lets group members know what is expected of them," and #7) "He/she makes sure that his/her part in the group is understood by group members."

The similarities in these items for both Carol and Jim indicate that these items are describing organizational norms —or at least departmental norms. The employees of this department are highly educated and are doing work which is *not* highly routinized. Hence they would not be asked to conform to standardized procedures. On the contrary, the comments made by interviewees indicate that taking initiative and tackling new problems are positive values in this work group.

CONCLUSION

Critical incidents emerged in the interviews with the co-workers of each of the four business leaders. The nature of these incidents provides an essential clue to the stereotyped images of male and female leaders that co-workers maintain. Evaluations of the leaders' behavior in the incidents gives an indication of how they are compared and contrasted to the stereotyped images.

For Dan Monroe, manager of retail sales of a small business, the critical incident was a failure to speak up to his boss, the owner of the business, for one of his subordinates. This incident symbolized his deviance from the tough male leader stereotype. Subsequently he was considered to be a weak leader. His leadership style profile looks like a caricature of so-called "feminine" submissiveness. His score on the Role Assumption Subscale was the lowest of the twelve leaders who participated in the study.

For Eileen Grant, manager of commercial sales of the same small business, the critical incident was her unexplained absences from the office. This behavior raised the spectre of the uncommitted female worker. Co-workers expressed concern about her dependability and the "bad example" she was setting.

For Jim Stevens, project director in a large industrial corporation, the critical incident involved the loss of staff members who were transferred to another project. Although theoretically such personnel changes are proper operating prcedure for a matrix organization, in reality the transfer was viewed as a sign of weakness. Jim was reportedly not "tough" enough to hang on to his good people. In spite of many years of seniority and an accumulation of expertise, Jim's Role Assumption score was the second lowest of the twelve leaders in the study.

For Carol Victor, an attractive, young project director working in the same industrial corporation (which has the *least* positive atitudes toward women as leaders of the organizations included in the study, and the *least* experience employing women), the critical incidents were those numerous "situations that come up" under such circumstances. The adept way in which Carol dealt with these situations helped to earn her the highest rating on the Role Assumption Subscale of the twelve leaders in the study. Evidently these incidents provided her with the opportunity to demonstrate her deviance from the sex-object stereotype that her appearance evoked.[5]

The notion that sex-role stereotypes function as a standard against which leaders are evaluated was illustrated in Chapter One with the case of Georgia Rosenbloom. In the cases of Eileen and Carol, the stereotypes are also negative. A good manager does not lack commitment to the job, nor is she a sex-object. In order to be evaluated as a good manager, these women have to prove themselves to be different from a variety of images of the incompetent lady boss.

In the cases of the male managers, Dan and Jim, the sex-role stereotype provides a positive standard. Both a good manager and a male manager are expected to be strong, tough and aggressive. In order to be evaluated as a good manager, these men must not deviate too much from this image. *One could say that the women are perceived as incompetent until proven capable, while the men are perceived as capable until proven incompetent.*

Both the female and the male leaders in these cases are victimized by sex-role stereotypes—victimized in the sense that their freedom is limited. Eileen Grant's freedom to leave the office for a legitimate reason that she had the right to keep confidential is limited by the stereotype of the female worker as lacking commitment to her job. Dan Monroe's and Jim Stevens' freedom to lead in a style that is softer and less aggressive is limited by the stereotype of the male leader as being always tough.

The concept, "role encapsulation," has been used to describe the limits placed on "tokens" i.e., women or men or minority group members who work in a group composed predominantly of people who are different from themselves. In *Men and Women of the Corporation,* Kanter (1977a, p. 230) states that "such stereotypical assumptions about what tokens 'must' be like, such mistaken attributions and biased judgements, tend to force tokens into playing limited and caricatured roles." Both the female and the male leaders described in the cases above are similarly limited by stereotyping.

In discussing her study of women in traditionally male occupations, e.g., craft technician, and men in traditionally female occupations, e.g., clerical worker, Carol Tropp Schreiber (1979, p. 119) applies the concept of role encapsulation to both women and men in the position of being a token group member. Schreiber (1979, p. 119) concludes that "Such token male roles as achievers and bosses may represent counterparts to female roles as mascot, seductress, iron maiden and mother." Role encapsulation is not just a "women's problem."

Leaders share many of the structural characteristics of tokens. They are highly visible members of their organizations. They are different in status from other members of their work groups, i.e., their subordinates, and therefore, bear some social isolation. Because they are important members of the organization, co-workers are anxious to make sense of the leaders' behavior. Encapsulating the leader in a sex-role stereotype is one way of doing so.

Once the encapsulating stereotype is questioned—and one can assume that many repetitions of deviant behavior must occur before the stereotype may begin to be doubted—then the deviance may be seen as extreme. Hence Carol Victor who disproves the notion that attractive women are not managerial material is viewed as an extraordinarily good leader indeed. Or for Dan Monroe, who has failed to match the tough male leader image, his style profile is a caricature of the weak, submissive leader.

Furthermore, subordinates and co-workers are able to enforce the encapsulation of the leaders in their stereotyped images. The leaders pay the consequences of censure (or reward) that co-workers impose. Eileen Grant paid for not avoiding the negative stereotype of the uncommitted female worker. Dan and Jim paid for not conforming to the positive image of the strong and aggressive male leader. Carol Victor

enjoyed the praise that she earned by disspelling the notion
that attractive women are not good managers.

The importance of sex-role stereotypes to the success of
these leaders is obvious. Eileen Grant was aware that she
was being criticized for her absences and felt uncomfortable
but saw no alternatives in dealing with the situation. Dan
was not so aware of the criticism directed at him. He knew
that he lacked credibility and authority with his subordinates,
however, and felt vaguely dissatisfied with his job. Both
managers suffered in terms of personal stress, job satisfaction and effectiveness in their organization.

When all twelve leaders of the study are considered as a
single group, statistics indicate that liberation from stereotypes is beneficial to men as well as women. Co-workers who
have more positive attitudes toward women as leaders
perceive male leaders differently than co-workers who have
less positive attitudes toward women as leaders. Specifically, people who have more positive attitudes toward women
as leaders tend to rate male leaders higher on role assumption and initiation of structure and lower on submissiveness.[6]
One interpretation of this finding is that the more "liberated"
a worker is, the broader is the conception of acceptable male
leadership behavior.

Because the two business organizations in which Dan,
Eileen, Jim and Carol work have the least positive attitudes
toward women, one could assume that the leaders are encapsulated in the narrowest, most traditional versions of the sex-
role stereotypes. One could also speculate that these leaders
are the most firmly encapsulated in the leadership images of
their co-workers. Analysis of the information on the leaders
of the educational and social service organizations in subsequent chapters will address this issue.

According to Kurt Lewin's (1951) model of change, the
first step is the "unfreezing" of old ideas. Chapters Three
and Four will explore the question of how the traditional
myths concerning women and men as leaders may be
unfreezing in organizations which have more experience with
female leadership. As stereotyping comes to be seen as
limiting both women and men in achieving their potential as
leaders, this aspect of women's liberation becomes clearly
one of human liberation.

NOTES

1. Eileen Grant and all other names of individuals and organizations are fictitious. The purpose of the fictious names is to protect the confidentiality of the participants of the study.

2. Peters, L. H., Terborg, J. R., and Taynor, J., Women as Managers Scale: A Measure of Attitudes Toward Women in Management Positions. *JSAS Catalog of Selected Documents in Psychology*, 1974, 4. (See Appendix on Instrumentation for information on this instrument).

3. La Forge, R., and Suczek, R., "The Interpersonal Dimension of Personality: III. an Interpersonal Check List." *Journal of Personality*, 1955, 24 (1), 94-112.

4. Ohio State Leadership Studies and Bureau of Business Research. Leader Behavior Description Questionnaire—Form XII. Columbus: Ohio State University, 1962. (See Appendix on Instrumentation for information on this instrument.)

5. Heilman, M. E., "Sometimes Beauty Can Be Beastly." *The New York Times*, Sunday, June 22, 1980. In this article, Professor Heilman reports on a study which indicates that while attractiveness is an advantage for women seeking non-managerial positions, it is actually a disadvantage for women being considered for managerial positions.

6. For male leaders, co-workers' attitudes toward women as leaders correlated significantly with Role Assumption scores ($r = .33$, $p < .05$), with Initiation of Structure scores ($r = .34$, $p < .05$), and with the style variable, submissiveness ($r = -.36$, $p < .05$).

CHAPTER THREE: WOMEN AND MEN WHO LEAD—
EDUCATIONAL ORGANIZATIONS

"Our main hope for disenthralling ourselves from our overemphasis on power lies . . . in seeing that the most powerful influences consist of deeply human relationships in which two or more persons *engage* with one another. It lies in a more realistic, a more sophisticated understanding of power, and of the often far more consequential exercise of mutual persuasion, exchange, elevation, and transformation—in short of leadership."

James MacGregor Burns, *Leadership*

"The evidence suggests clearly that it is not enough for an administrator to be concerned with human relations only . . . In addition the administrator must be able to help a staff develop goals and a plan of action, he must be able to help each staff member see where he can make his particular contribution to the total effort and he must stimulate each staff member to make his contribution the best of which he is capable."

Roald F. Campbell, Edwin M. Bridges and Ralph O. Nystrand, *Introduction to Educational Administration*

"He has tremendous humanistic qualities.   He is a professional." Paul Meyer, administrator for the school district, was
described in these glowing terms by a member of his staff.
Humanistic and professional are terms which convey the
highest possible praise to an educational administator.   Just as
strong and rational are the bottom line of business administration, professional and humane are the bottom line of
education administration.[1]   Such terms are appropriate for
organizations whose primary purpose is to service the educational needs of children and young adults.

Both of these qualities, professionalism and humanity,
imply stereotypically feminine leadership qualities. According
to the professional orientation, the teacher or administrator's
primary loyalty is to the profession rather than to the
employing organization.   Responsibility is first of all to the
clients who in this case are the students.   The professional is
expected to be self-controlled and not to require close supervision.   He or she is capable of making independent decisions
based on the principles that professional training has imbued
(Hoy and Miskel, 1978).

Supervising such a group of professionals would require a
non-authoritarian leadership style.   Subordinates would be
approached in an egalitarian manner, as a group of colleagues.
Supervision would be loose enough to allow subordinates to
make their own decisions and mistakes.   In short, subordinates
would be treated like professionals.   Since women are stereotypically more egalitarian and less authoritarian than men (see
Chapter One), wouldn't educational administration be a likely
job for a woman?

Humanistic education (sometimes called "affective education") is a more recent school of thought which, like professionalism, values feminine qualities.   The basic premise of
humanistic education is that students should be educated as
whole human beings.   Schools should be places where emotions
are dealt with as well as intellects.

Another major aspect of humanistic education is a focus
on "process" or on teaching students how to learn.   This
approach contrasts with traditional education where the
emphasis is on the product or content (measured in quantitative terms) of the learnings (Kirschenbaum and Simon, 1974).
Focusing on emotions, on process or the human side of
enterprise are orientations which are stereotypically feminine.

In spite of these ideologies, the same pyramid-shaped distribution of women employees has existed in educational as in business organizations: women have been concentrated at the lower levels of the organizations with the administrative or leadership ranks being largely male. In response to the question of whether different things have helped men and women to advance in the organization, one respondent from the school district reported: "For a long time the men were the ones who got all the administrative positions." Another repondent was more specific in describing how the ladder is climbed: "Back fifteen to seventeen years ago, you belonged to the _____ Men's Club which gave you a chance to be looked at [for promotion]. Phi Delta Kappa [the education honor society] just opened up two or three years ago to women." Similarly, the concentration of women in the lower positions in institutions of higher education is well documented (Howard, 1978).

In sum, the educational organizations are by some measures more liberated in their attitudes toward women than the business organizations. They have ideologies which support the so-called feminine styles of nonauthoritarian and humanistic leadership. They have somewhat greater experience than business organizations with women in positions of leadership. They score higher than the business organizations on the measure of attitudes toward women which was used in this study (Peters, Terborg and Taynor, 1974).

In spite of these advances for women, evidence of the male bias in leadership remains. This bias is brought out in the cases of Paul Meyer, Mary Duncan, Herb Weiss and Rose Lerner. A look at these leaders and the way in which sex role stereotypes affect their work lives follows.

PUBLIC SCHOOL DISTRICT

Mary Duncan and Paul Meyer are administrators in an urban public school district. They both began their careers as school teachers and worked their way up into the administrative ranks. Together they are responsible for the training of teaching and non-teaching personnel for the school district. Each administrator supervises a staff of trainers who implement the training actitivies in schools throughout the city. Their bosses are assistants to the Superintendent of Schools.

A comparison of the style profiles for administrators Meyer and Duncan reveals that the greatest difference is in the affiliative dimension. Mary Duncan's profile is the stereotypically more affiliative. She is also the more dominant leader. Her profile is an example of the mother stereotype: highly affiliative and dominant (see Figure 3-1).

Compared to his female counterpart, Paul Meyer's profile is an example of moderation in leadership style. Mary's profile exceeds Paul's on all four style dimensions: dominance, affiliation, submission and hostility. The one aspect of Paul's profile which is surprising (for a man) is his relatively high score on the "docile" variable. In the information about Paul which follows, this score is shown to be related to the greatly admired humanistic and professional qualities of this leader.

Paul Meyer, Administrator

Paul Meyer is a forty-nine year old white administrator. His entire career has been at the school district where he has worked for twenty-seven years. At the time that Paul participated in the leadership study, he was about to be promoted to superintendent of one of the divisions of the school district.

Paul's age, forty-nine, is average for his work group where ages range from thirty to fifty-seven. His seniority is also typical. The average number of years in the organization is twenty-one. Paul's boss is fifty-seven years old and has worked for the school district for thirty-six years. Seniority is obviously very important for advancement in this organization.

Educational level is another factor which figures into consideration for promotion. All of Paul's co-workers have done graduate work on either the master's or doctoral level. One of Paul's subordinates has a doctorate, two of his peers hold doctoral degrees and his boss has a doctorate. Paul himself has a master's degree.

Paul is married and has one child. His wife works outside the home more than twenty hours a week. With the exception of one peer who is separated, all of Paul's co-workers are married. Lifestyles of co-workers vary, however, in terms of family size and the extent to which spouses work outside the home.

FIGURE 3-1

Public School District

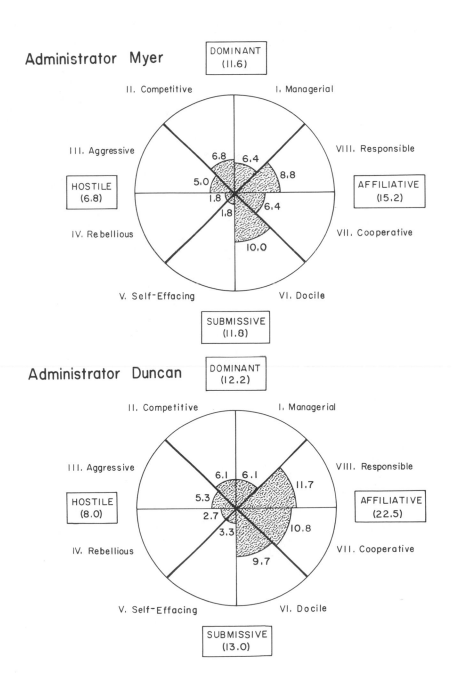

Administrator Myer

DOMINANT
(11.6)

II. Competitive   I. Managerial

III. Aggressive   VIII. Responsible

6.8   6.4
5.0   8.8
HOSTILE   AFFILIATIVE
(6.8)   1.8   (15.2)
1.8   6.4

IV. Rebellious   VII. Cooperative

10.0

V. Self-Effacing   VI. Docile

SUBMISSIVE
(11.8)

Administrator Duncan

DOMINANT
(12.2)

II. Competitive   I. Managerial

III. Aggressive   VIII. Responsible

6.1   6.1
11.7
5.3
HOSTILE   AFFILIATIVE
(8.0)   2.7   (22.5)
3.3   10.8

IV. Rebellious   VII. Cooperative

9.7

V. Self-Effacing   VI. Docile

SUBMISSIVE
(13.0)

Although racially and sexually mixed, Paul's work group is predominantly white and male. Of the eight people who participated in the study, one subordinate is black. One subordinate and one peer are women. Hence, Paul Meyer is typical of his colleagues in being white, male, middle-aged, married, and educated beyond the undergraduate level.

Listening to co-workers describe Paul Meyer's strengths as a leader, it becomes clear that he is not merely competent, he has a special quality that enables him to unlock the potential of those who work for him. Like a master teacher, he helps his subordinates to stretch and grow. In the words of one of his co-workers: "It's been a great experience working for the man. He has tremendous humanistic qualities going for him." "He's a fine administrator." "He's a truly professional person through and through." "He's very human in his approaches."

Other co-workers are more specific in describing Paul's special ability to relate to people. Part of this ability is listening skill. "He listens to other people. He's appreciative of ideas from others." One happy consequence of Paul's listening ability is that he appears to be approachable. "He makes you feel at ease in going to him with any problem you may have." Another consequence is that co-workers feel respected as individuals: "He respects the decisions you make." "He uses good psychology. If a person is interested in experimenting, he'll allow it. If he sees that the person is not interested, he'll set limits." Yet another consequence of Paul's ability to listen is that co-workers feel his concern for them as human beings—not just producers of work.

Another part of Paul's humanity is a non-authoritarian leadership style. In supervising individual workers he "suggests, but won't impose." When working in a group, he participates in an egalitarian manner, or "as a peer." He "never dominates" a group. One co-worker describes his behavior in work groups: "He's very thoughtful. He sits back, waits, listens, then comes out with an astute observation." These comments help explain the relatively high "docile" score of Paul's style profile. He can be "laid back" enough to allow others to be heard.

Another part of Paul's success lies in his ability to motivate. In the words of one of his subordinates, "You want to work for him. He wants to motivate you to do the best you can."

Co-workers are careful to point out, however, that Paul's humanity and sensitivity are not excessively emotional. He does not have volatile moods. He, rather, "exudes calmness." He also keeps an appropriate and compatible distance between himself and his subordinates; "He's not a buddy." However open, he keeps his work relationships business-like.

In addition to Paul's extraordinary interpersonal strengths, he has many of the usual competencies of leadership. He is experienced and knowlegeable in his field. He is resourceful when the limits of his expertise are reached. He is hard-working and "given to successful completion of tasks." His boss states that "he is dedicated and sets an example of dedication." He is an "excellent speaker," expected to be well prepared and informative. Finally, Paul is well-organized. According to his boss, Paul is "analytical when working on problems."

The recognition of Paul's success as a leader is universal. Still, his deviation from the tough, aloof and rational male stereotype occasionally causes conflict for co-workers. Paul's boss describes the leader's weakness as "not making decisions quickly enough." One co-worker states that Paul is "too nice . . . too concerned about people's feelings." Another co-worker expresses ambivalent feelings about Paul's leader-ship style: "He's far more tolerant of people than I would be. [This is] really a strengh. Some people think he's too lenient yet they don't take advantage." This co-worker is surprised at the success of such a "lenient" or non authoritarian style of leadership, a style which deviates from the tough and aloof male stereotype.

It is not surprising that this highly praised leader ranked second (of the twelve leaders in the study) on the Role Assumption Subscale. He received the highest possible scores on two items: #5) "He (never) is the leader of the group in name only" and #8) "He takes full charge when emergencies arise." The next highest items are #6) "He (never) backs down when he ought to stand firm" and #10) "He is easily recognized as the leader of the group." This humanistic leader is clearly seen as being a strong leader.

Another piece of evidence for Paul's strength as a leader comes from the Initiating Structure Subscale. Paul's score was the highest of the twelve leaders in the study ($\overline{X}$ = 4.6). On four items he received the highest possible score. These items echo the comments of his co-workers concerning the openness of his relationships with them: #1) "He lets group members know what is expected of them," #4) "He makes his attitudes clear to the group," #7) "He makes sure his part in the group is understood by group members," and #9) "He maintains definite standards of performance."

The lowest item on Paul's Initiating Structure Subscale underlines co-workers' comments concerning the latitude he gives his subordinates: #5) "He decides what shall be done and how it shall be done."

Mary Duncan, Administrator

Mary Duncan is a fifty-nine year old white administrator who describes her leadership style as "motherly." Mary has accumulated twenty-three years of seniority in the school district and raised three children. She is married, has a master's degree and is taking courses toward a doctorate.

Mary's work situation shows the scars of an era in which women were rarely promoted. All of the subordinates who participated in the study are women (two are black, two are white). In contrast, all of the peers as well as Mary's boss are white males.

Mary's work group is also less educated than Paul's group of co-workers. There are no doctoral degrees held by Mary's co-workers. Educational levels range from "high school education or less" (Mary's secretary) to "some graduate work or master's degree."

Mary's boss is younger than herself and has less seniority. He is forty-four and has ten years of work experience in the school district.

Similar to Paul Meyer's group of co-workers, Mary's group is relatively old and senior. Ages of co-workers range from thirty-five to sixty-two with an average age of forty-nine. Years of service to the organization range from six to thirty-one with an average of twelve.

In terms of lifestyle, the group is homogeneous. All except one widow are married. All except the youngest co-worker (thirty-three years old) have children. All spouses except for one who works part-time (less than twenty hours per week), work outside the home more than twenty hours per week.

In sum, Mary's work group has certain signs of being lower status than Paul's. As a group the co-workers are less educated and more female. The comments given in interviews concerning Mary Duncan's strengths and weaknesses as a leader bear out the notion that she is somewhat less successful as a leader than her male counterpart, Paul Meyer.

Mary abides by the work ethic and is complimented by co-workers on being hard-working: "She's very determined. Nothing's too hard for her to do because she loves her work." "She's a conscientious worker, goes above the call of duty." "She's a very responsible person."

Mary's hard work is also well-organized. Her boss comments that "as a leader she is fantastic at taking charge of projects and giving them leadership and follow-through. She has an excellent eye for detail."

One consequence of her well-organized state is that she has knowledge and information available when needed. She is viewed as being able to "think quickly" and as "having answers when needed." One of her peers comments: "She's very knowledgeable about her work. I frequently call on her for some obscure regulation."

Furthermore, Mary can communicate her knowledge. "She makes an excellent presentation, has a flair for public speaking." She is well-connected and well-liked outside of her own office too.

Finally, Mary has humanistic qualities. She is described as being a "kind person" who "tries very hard to make the work situation comfortable for everyone." Like her male counterpart, Paul Meyer, she is a good listener, "open to different views." She can even "listen thoroughly to individual complaints and evalute them carefully before making a decision." Like her female stereotype, "She's democratic and wants everyone's ideas to be heard. She allows her subordinates to grow in their respective positions."

Mary's "feminine" virtues are sometimes viewed as excessive, as signs of weakness. She is haunted by a mother stereotype, the mother who wants so much to be liked that she loses the distance from subordinates and the assertiveness required for leadership—a mother who is too soft. She "tries to please everyone." "She is such a kind individual that some people may take advantage of her." "She'll change her whole goal if someone is stronger or more forceful than her." According to her boss, Mary "tends to bend over backwards to accommodate people."

A particular dilemma that results from her kindly ways is that Mary finds it difficult to say "no" to work assignments. In trying to please everyone she "tries to tackle too many things, tries to overdo." Her boss reports that she "cannot delegate enough to other people."

Mary's strengths as an organizer, an expert, a hard working responsible person are evident in the two highest items of the Role Assumption Subscale: #5) "She is (never) the leader of the group in name only." And #10) "She is easily recognized as leader of the group."

Her weakness concerning excessive use of democratic procedures and lack of assertion of her own position is validated by the two items which received the lowest scores: #1) "She is (never) hesitant about taking initiative in the group," and #9) "She overcomes attempts to challenge her leadership." Mary's overall score on the Role Assumption Subscale was lower than Paul's. (Of the twelve leaders in the study, she ranked ninth and he ranked second.)

Mary's overall score on the Initiating Structure Subscale is similar to the score that Paul received. (Paul's score was the highest of the twelve leaders and Mary's score ranked second.) The similarity in their scores indicates that high levels of structure are simply normal for this organization, and do not differentiate between the styles of these two leaders.

The figures which do provide information about the leadership style of Mary Duncan are the scores on individual items of the Initiating Structure Subscale. Mary's two highest items are identical to two of Paul's highest items: #1) "She lets group members know what is expected of them," and #7) "She makes sure that her part in the group is understood by group members." Even on these items Mary's scores were lower than Paul's. In fact, Mary scored lower on all items of this subscale with the exception of two items: #2) "She encourages the use of uniform procedures," and #5) "She decides what shall be done and how it shall be done." These items are interesting because they concur with the positive comments of Paul's co-workers concerning his tendency to give large amounts of leeway to his subordinates in the performance of their work. By comparison Mary appears to be overbearing in her supervision, like a doting mother.

URBAN UNIVERSITY

Herb Weiss and Rose Lerner are both department chairpersons in urban universities. They are in different academic subject fields, but each leader is within a college of arts and sciences. In addition to teaching they are responsible for the adminis- trative duties of their respective departments. These duties include hiring new faculty members, implementing the depart- ment's budget, reporting and advocating the department's needs and activities to their boss, the dean of the college, as well as to other department heads and administrators of the university.

A look at these leaders' style profiles indicates that they are both relatively high on the affiliative dimension. (Of the twelve leaders, Weiss ranked first and Lerner third on this dimension.) Weiss is the more affiliative of the pair and also the more dominant. His situation is similar to Mary Duncan's, i.e., she is more affiliative and more dominant than her male counterpart, Paul Meyer. Weiss' profile also fits the mother stereotype. The fact that Weiss is the male of this pair of leaders does not fit the stereotype of the affiliative female.

Herb Weiss, Chairperson

Herb Weiss is firmly established in his organization. He is fifty-six years old and white. He has worked for the university for the past twenty-four years. He holds a doctoral degree and is tenured in his department. Therefore, he cannot be fired except for extraordinary reasons. He expects to retire from his current position when he reaches the appropriate age.

Consistent with university employment policies, Herb's co-workers are also highly educated. With two exceptions, all of his co-workers who participated in the study hold doctoral degrees. One exception is a subordinate who has a master's degree, and the other exception is Herb's secretary who has a high school education.

Herb is not the oldest of his work group. Aside from his boss who is sixty-three, one subordinate is fifty-seven, one is sixty-one, and one peer is his age, fifty-six. The average age for the group is fifty-one with ages ranging from thirty-two to sixty-three.

Herb's leadership position is strengthened by being the member of his work group with by far the most seniority. His

FIGURE 3-2

Urban University

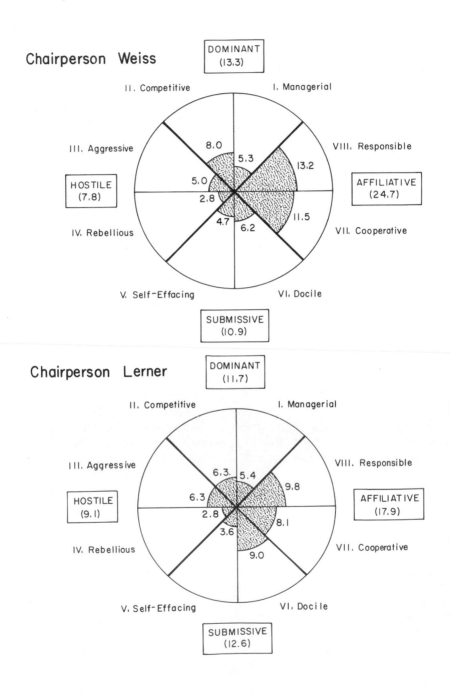

Chairperson Weiss

DOMINANT
(13.3)

II. Competitive   I. Managerial

III. Aggressive   VIII. Responsible

8.0
5.3
13.2

HOSTILE
(7.8)

5.0
2.8

AFFILIATIVE
(24.7)

4.7
6.2
11.5

IV. Rebellious   VII. Cooperative

V. Self-Effacing   VI. Docile

SUBMISSIVE
(10.9)

Chairperson Lerner

DOMINANT
(11.7)

II. Competitive   I. Managerial

III. Aggressive   VIII. Responsible

6.3
5.4
9.8

HOSTILE
(9.1)

6.3
2.8

AFFILIATIVE
(17.9)

3.6
8.1

9.0

IV. Rebellious   VII. Cooperative

V. Self-Effacing   VI. Docile

SUBMISSIVE
(12.6)

boss has just ten years at the university. The person who is closest to Herb in terms of seniority is a subordinate who has been in the organization for thirteen years. The average number of years of seniority is ten with a range from two to twenty-four years.

Lifestyles of Herb's work group are diverse. Some people are married, others have never been married and others are divorced. Numbers of children range from none to four. With the exception of Herb's boss whose wife works part-time, all other spouses work outside the home more than twenty hours a week. Herb himself is married and has three children. His wife works outside the home full-time.

Several comments of Herb's co-workers relate to the extremely high affiliative score of his style profile. (Herb's was the highest score on this dimension of all twelve leaders of the study.) Co-workers view this attribute of Herb as a strength. In their words, "He is very personable. He gets along well with his staff." Another co-worker phrased her praise very simply: "I like him." However extreme this quality appears on the style profile, Herb is not criticized for personalizing work issues, for bringing personal problems to work, or for being too emotionally involved in his work.

Herb's affiliative style is also appreciated by co-workers because he is pleasantly nonauthoritarian. While maintaining his "strong character," he does not use authoritarian strategies. Several co-workers complimented Herb on his democratic way of conducting faculty meetings: "He seems to handle himself very well [at faculty meetings]. He's obviously the superior when moderating meetings or general discussions. He keeps things organized without being authoritarian." "He can do the leadership job [i.e., running meetings] very well."

Another basis of Herb's authority, his seniority, is alluded to in co-workers' comments. Herb has that quality of the male stereotype described in Chapter One: He "comes from experience and self-confidence." The years of seniority in the organization and the tenured status give Herb an aspect of strength.

The one weakness that is attributed to Herb is a failure to "fight with the higher authority in the school or with other department heads." While he is viewed as a strong leader within his department, he does not exert his influence outside in the broader area of university politics.

Other criticisms of Herb which were not verbalized in the interviews are brought out in the items of the Role Assumption Subscale. Herb's overall score ranked fifth among the twelve leaders of the study. His two lowest items indicate that there may be some criticism of his extremely affiliative style which were not verbalized in the interviews:[2] item #4) "He (never) lets some members take advantage of him," and Item #1) "He is (never) hesitant about taking initiative in the group."

The next lowest items relate to his failure to assert himself in the university community outside the department: #2) "He (never) fails to take necessary action," and #6) "He (never) backs down when he ought to stand firm."

Whatever the criticisms of Herb's leadership may be, he is clearly a strong and undisputed leader. The item which received the highest score on Herb's Role Assumption Subscale is #5) "He is (never) the leader of the group in name only."

As on the Role Assumption Subscale, Herb's rank on the initiating Structure Subscale was moderate. (He ranked fourth.) The lowest items of this scale underline the democratic nature of his style: #3) "He tries out his ideas in the group," and #5) "He decides what shall be done and how it shall be done." He does not interject or impose his own opinions or will on his subordinates.

Rose Lerner, Chairperson

Compared to her male counterpart, Herb Weiss, Rose Lerner is a newcomer to her profession. She has been in her current position just two years. Furthermore, this job is the first position she has held since completing her doctoral degree. Rose shies away from the word "leader," conceiving of herself as a facilitator of her new department.

Rose is the same age as Herb Weiss, i.e., fifty-six. Her co-workers, however, are somewhat younger and less senior than the co-workers of Herb. Her co-workers range in age from twenty-eight to sixty-three with an average age of forty-five. Years of seniority range from one to twenty-one with an average of five years at the university. Because the department that Rose chairs is newly created (she was hired to develop the department), all of her subordinates have been hired during the past year or two.

Rose's co-workers are heterogeneous in terms of race, sex, marital status, number of children, and the extent to which spouses work outside the home. Of the co-workers participating in the study, no single race, sex, or lifestyle represents the majority. The group is truly diverse. Rose herself is a widow and has one child.

The one characteristic which the group has in common is a high level of education. With the exception of two secretaries, all of Rose's co-workers have either master's or doctoral degrees. The two co-workers with master's degrees are subordinates.

In sum, Rose's job appears to be challenging. She is building a new department from its inception. She is working with a very diverse group of people. She is new both to the ranks of the Ph. D.'s and to the college in which she is employed. On the other hand, she has the authority which comes with being a newcomer from the outside, the prestige of being hired explicitly to start up a new program.

How does she fare? Comments from co-workers indicate that the egalitarian stereotype haunts Rose in her leadership role. Some aspects of this style are viewed as strengths. She is complimented on "treating everyone equal" and on using "participatory planning" where the staff has input. The advantage of this egalitarian style is that decisions are well informed: "She draws on staff and others possessing expertise."

An egalitarian style of leadership relies heavily on the maintenance of good staff relations, and Rose is able to achieve this goal. She reportedly "relates well to staff." She has a good enough rapport with them that she can even critique her staff effectively. Rose's rapport with her staff has an additional charismatic quality: "Her leadership is contagious. You get involved with her interests."

Rose also leads by example. She is complimented on her "commitment to her work." Her behavior provides a model of hard work and dedication for her staff.

Finally, Rose's leadership is based on expertise. Her job of establishing a new department requires extensive interaction with the university administration outside of her own department. In performing this aspect of her job, she is complimented on her "good knowledge of university structure." She knows her way around the system.

Criticisms of Rose's performance of her leadership role focus on her participatory decision-making style. Some criticisms are mild, suggesting that minor improvements in the decision-making model are necessary. One comment is that Rose needs "tighter planning for meetings" to make her decision-making process more effective. Another comment is that she "draws too much on others."

A somewhat stronger criticism of Rose's decision-making style comes from co-workers who think that she is simply indecisive: "She can put things off, doesn't make decisions." Another co-workers describes her indecisiveness: "[She thinks] the decision will take care of itself. She's not clearly taking responsibility."

The strongest criticism of Rose's decision-making style is voiced by one of her peers: "She likes group approval rather than being a leader. In some circumstances it works well but generally someone ultimately takes a stand. So far she's been able to get a consensus." In the mind of that observer, decision-making by means of group consensus is not real leadership.

Another weakness attributed to Rose's leadership is related to the female stereotype: "She tends to get over-emotional, to see too much as a crisis." One can surmise that from Rose's viewpoint a crisis requires a full department meeting with all staff members participating in the resolution of the crisis. Hence her frequent use of the participatory decision-making process.

These criticisms undermine Rose's authority and stature as a leader in spite of the competence that is seen in her ratings on the Role Assumption Subscale. Her overall score ranks third among the twelve leaders of the study. Her rank is comparatively higher than the rank of Herb Weiss, her male counterpart. (His rank was fifth.)

The two highest items of this subscale support the notion that her leadership has strengths in spite of criticisms of her participatory decision-making style: #5) "She is (never) the leader of the group in name only," and #10) "She is easily recognized as the leader of the group."

Her ability to act as group leader in the frequent department meetings is supported by the next highest items: #3) "She (never) lets other persons take away her leadership in the group," and #9) "She overcomes attempts to challenge her leadership."

An even more meaningful assessment of Rose's leadership can be made by comparing her scores on the Initiating

Structure Subscale with the ratings of Herb Weiss. Although the overall scores of the two leaders is identical ($\overline{X}$ = 4.2 for both Herb and Rose), their ratings on several individual items differ substantially. Rose's highest items validate her skill as a group facilitator: #3) "She tries out her ideas in the group," and #9) "She maintains definite standards of performance." A close second in terms of ratings are items #1) "She lets group members know what is expected of them," #4) "She makes her attitude clear to the group," and #7) "She makes sure that her part in the group is understood by group members." On all but the last item (#7) Rose's score was *higher* than Herb's.

The item on which the two leader's scores were most discrepant, however, was #2) "He/she encourages the use of uniform procedures." This item was Rose's lowest and one of Herb's highest. Rose, the egalitarian, would not be expected to institute uniform procedures. Her extremely low score on this item (2.8) supports the comments of her co-workers that her reliance on group consensus for decision-making is extreme. The item also is indicative of the circumstances of her leadership, i.e., a new department which is still establishing itself would not yet have uniform procedures to follow. By this measure, Herb is the more authoritarian of the pair.

CONCLUSION

In these organizations with traditions of democratic and humanistic education and of academic freedom, one would expect the images of leadership to be feminine. In organizations whose purpose is to educate children and young adults—a function of motherhood—one would expect sensitivity and gentleness to be valued. Women are stereotypically the egalitarian and humane sex. Women are also less likely to be authoritarian.

What then is the model of leadership which emerges from these four educational leaders? The positive valuing of sensitivity, democracy, humanity is evident in the descriptions of all four of the educational leaders. Paul Meyer is complimented on being humanistic in the true sense of the word. His relationships with his staff have an inspirational quality which motivates subordinates to achieve their potential as professionals and as human beings. His willingness and ability to listen are widely praised as indications of his sensitivity. The positive valuing of these attributes is evident in Paul's rank, second, on the Role Assumption Subscale.

Mary Duncan is also seen as having the strength of listening skills and sensitivity to others. Furthermore, Mary is viewed as a "kind" person, concerned even about the psychological comfort of her employees. In contrast to Paul, however, Mary ranks ninth on the Role Assumption Scale, and is consistenly criticized for lack of assertion, as well as excessive involvement and concern for her employees.

Herb Weiss is unanimously praised for his nonauthoritarian style of conducting staff meetings and his personable ways. There is strong evidence, however, that Herb's affiliativeness may be extreme. His score is the highest of all twelve leaders on the affiliative dimension of the style profile. His co-workers report that he avoids conflict and does not assert himself outside the department in the university political arena.

Nonetheless, Herb is viewed as a fairly strong leader who organizes and maintains control. He appears to be experienced and self-confident. Herb's score on the Role Assumption Subscale is moderate.

Rose Lerner, like Paul Meyer of the school district, is able to engage her subordinates and motivate them. She is not only a good listener but she is also able to provide her staff with feedback—even constructive criticism. She is able to utilize the resources of co-workers in a process of group decision-making. She ranks third on the Role Assumption Subscale.

Yet Rose is severely criticized for her democratic decision-making style. Admonitions range from mild skepticism concerning the workability of such a process to stern accusations of indecisiveness and lack of leadership. Rose is also described as over-emotional and given to defining all problems as crises requiring participative decision-making processes.

The valuing of the so-called feminine leadership qualities —sensitivity, democracy, and humanity—exists without regard for gender. Women and men alike are praised and admired by co-workers for demonstrating these attributes. The climate and ideological foundations of the educational organization override sex-role stereotypes in this regard.

Still, sex-role stereotypes have a significant effect on the worklives of these leaders. Paul and Herb are freer than the male business leaders to deviate from the tough macho image. (One can imagine how loudly Herb's affiliative style would be denounced in Dan Monroe's travel agency, for example.) Herb and Paul have been able to add on to a basically strong leadership the softer qualities of sensitivity and democracy.

The women, on the other hand, are still haunted by the traditional stereotypes. Rose's participatory style raises the spectre of the egalitarian who seeks the participation of others out of weakness. In spite of a consensus that Rose has many competencies as a leader, co-workers fear that she is not strong enough to make decisions independently.

Mary is similarly haunted by the mother image. "She is *so* strong," commented one of her subordinates. The tone of voice revealed the employee's conflict. Leaders are supposed to be strong and therefore strength should be a positive aspect of Mary's leadership. Yet Mary's stength did not feel good, it was of the doting mother variety. The stereotype of the mother lent a negative charge to her strength.

The male administrators are able to expand their repertoire of acceptable leader behaviors in this environment, to add on to the strong male leader image the softer qualities of sensitivity, and democracy. The women are not as able to expand their stereotyped roles. While their stereotypical virtues—sensitivity, humanity, and non authoritarian leadership—are readily recognized and praised by co-workers, the women are not able to expand their roles to include the traditionally male quality of strength. Rose's participatory decision-making style was assumed to be a sign of weakness and inability to act independently. Mary was cast as either the kind, sensitive, non-assertive mother or as the strong but doting and over-supervising mother.

The boundaries of role encapsulation are easier to extend for the men than for the women. Or, in Kurt Lewin's terms, there has been more unfreezing of the traditional myths about men as leaders than the traditional myths about women as leaders in these educational organizations.

NOTES

1. A small amount of research has documented differences in the conceptions of the effective business executive and the effective educational administrator (Powers, 1964; Miner,

1968).   Basically what these studies show is that "consideration," defined as "regards the comfort, well-being, status, and contributions of followers" (Ohio State Leadership Studies, 1962) is more important as an attribute of educational administrators than of business executives. In some cases the characteristics associated with success were opposites: Educational administrators who showed great consideration were considered to be the most promotable administrators. Business leaders who showed as much consideration, however, were considered to be "non promotables." They were too soft, too deviant from the tough male leader stereotype.

2.   In general, the university personnel who participated in the study were the least verbose and open in commenting on their leaders' strengths and weaknesses. Neither of the Deans or bosses of the department chairperson were available for interviewing.   Hence the comments concerning these leaders are somewhat abbreviated.   Pieced together with the information gleaned from the style profiles and the Role Assumption and Initiating Structure Subscales, however, the sparse comments of co-workers are enlightening nonetheless.

CHAPTER FOUR: WOMEN AND MEN WHO LEAD— SOCIAL SERVICE ORGANIZATIONS

"Although there is a definite preference for men as administrators, women have good opportunity to head agencies and organizations in the fields in which they predominate, notably in case work agencies. Women are employed exclusively as executives in group work agencies serving girls and women such as the Young Women's Christian Association, the Girl Scout organizations, and the Camp Fire Girls."

> Bulletin of the Women's Bureau, United States Department of Labor, 1951. *The Outlook for Women in Social Work Administration, Teaching and Research.*

"One may suspect that the dilemma Jane Addams faced in her education with the problems of undertaking some useful task in the world arose much more out of the fact that she was a woman—and an educated woman—than out of the course of study she had pursued. At that time men tended to place women of her cultivated tastes on a pedestal, and it seems likely that she had great difficulty in distinguishing the difference between a pedestal and a shelf."

Katherine A. Kendall,
Reflections on Social Work Education 1950-1978

Jane Addams is generally credited as being the founding mother of the social work profession. She was an educated woman who came to a poor neighborhood in Chicago where she successfully established and maintained a community center, Hull House. Jane Addams lived at Hull House for forty-six years, providing leadership in the reform of a wide range of social issues including public education, health, child labor, immigrant protection, women's rights, civil liberties and world peace. Her leadership was recognized by receipt of the Nobel Peace Prize in 1931 (Kendall, 1978).

Like Georgia Rosenbloom (see Chapter One), Jane Addams surprised the world with her leadership abilities. She may have begun her career as a charitable lady volunteering her time to do "good deeds" among the needy, yet she soon demonstrated that she had the traditionally male virtues of strength, unyielding principles, toughness in the face of her opponents and commitment to her work.

Even while engaging in tough battles for social reform, however, Jane Addams did not become an "iron maiden." She remained a lady in her loving and kind manner, in her readiness to listen to those who needed her, and in the democratic principles which governed Hull House (Kendall, 1978).

Out of the traditions which Jane Addams originated has grown a profession with a history of images of female leadership. No conflict exists between the work roles, nurturer and caretaker of the indigent and the ill and the sex role, woman. Furthermore, in recent years a commitment to equal employment opportunity for minority groups and women has become an important part of the ideology of the human service organization (Kerson and Alexander, 1979).

These traditions are certainly related to the fact that the social work profession is composed of approximately two-thirds women and one-third men (Chernesky, 1979). In spite of the psychological support these traditions provide, however, women are underrepresented in the administrative ranks of human service organizations. Furthermore, their numbers are declining. A survey of the Committee on Women's Issues of the National Association of Social Workers conducted in 1976 revealed that only 16 percent of 868 agencies surveyed had female directors. The study also revealed that the number of female directors had *decreased* bv 44 percent since the 1950s and was continuing to decline at a rate of 2 percent a year (Szakacs, 1977). The overrepresentation of men in the administrative ranks exists in a wide variety of different kinds of social service agencies, including family services, federal and state welfare organizations, juvenile correction facilities as well as in social and educational institutions (Kerson and Alexander, 1979, p. 315).

Obviously social service is not a utopia for female leadership. In the eyes of its female members, the profession of social work is not a place where women have "made it" in terms of assuming a fair or representative share of the leadership. Yet compared to the business and educational organizations represented in this study, the human service agency is a place where female leadership is relatively familiar and positively valued.[1] On a measure of attitudes toward women assuming managerial positions (Peters, Terborg and Taynor, 1974) employees of the social service agencies had the highest scores,[2] indicating the most positive attitudes toward women managers. Similarly, in a study of female supervisors in human service organizations, researchers found that employees "trained in Social Work agree more strongly (than employees with a different kind of training) that women are able managers. Those trained in Business and Public Administration indicated the least positive perceptions of women's managerial ability" (Ezell, Odewan and Sherman, 1980).

The status of sex stereotypes in this most liberated type of organization will be explored through agency directors Joe Ryan, Susan Baker, Ron Smith, and Anna Ferrari. Specifically, the following questions will be addressed: How do sex stereotypes function in this relatively "liberated" environment? Do sex stereotypes dissipate as some researchers suggest? Are the traditional images of women and men who lead still evident? Do the leaders who function in this more liberated climate have more freedom to lead in non-stereotyped ways?

STATE ALCOHOLISM CLINIC

Joe Ryan and Susan Baker are directors of alcoholism clinics. They have both come to their respective current positions from the Roman Catholic Church. Joe is a former priest, Susan a former nun. Their current positions represent their first jobs as members of the secular community.

The clinics are part of a state mental health department. Each clinic services one geographic district of a large metropolitan area. Joe and Susan are responsible for the entire operation of their clinics. Duties include hiring, firing, and supervising counseling staffs, lobbying for funds for the clinic and administering the clinic's budget.

The style profiles of Directors Ryan and Baker are the most stereotypypical of the six pairs of leaders (see Figure 4-1). Director Ryan, the man, is more dominant and less affiliative than his female counterpart, Director Baker. Joe Ryan is, indeed, the most dominant of the twelve leaders of the study. His profile is also higher than Susan's on every dimension except "affiliative," i.e., on "dominant," "hostile," and "submissive."

Joe Ryan, Clinic Director

Joe Ryan is forty-two years old. He was hired to direct the alcoholism clinic just one year ago. His qualifications for the job include his divinity degree and an additional master's degree in counseling psychology. Another qualification is his status as a reformed alcoholic.

Two of Joe's subordinates who participated in the study have also been working at the clinic for just one year. Another subordinate has been there for four years. Joe's peers, however, are more firmly established in the system in terms of seniority. One peer has been in the state mental health system for four years, another for six years, and another for fifteen years. By comparison, Joe's boss is similar to himself. He is forty-three years old and has been in the organization for three years.

In terms of age, sex, marital and family status, Joe's subordinates and peers are diverse. Ages range from twenty-eight to sixty-three. Co-workers consist of a balance of men and women. Lifestyles include singles, marrieds, remarrieds,

FIGURE 4-1

State Alcoholism Clinic

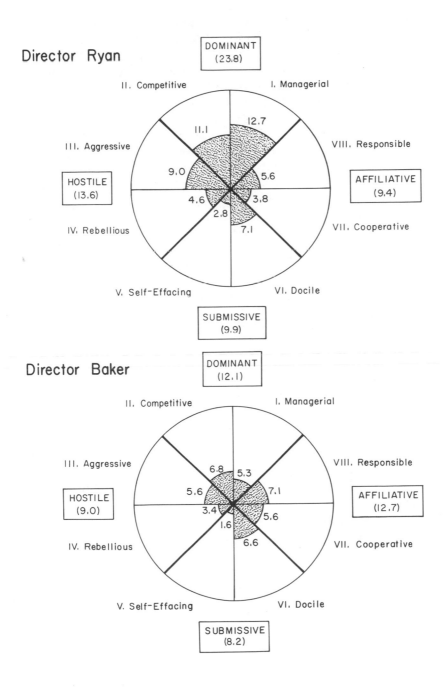

Director Ryan

DOMINANT
(23.8)

II. Competitive   I. Managerial

12.7

11.1

III. Aggressive   VIII. Responsible

9.0   5.6

HOSTILE   AFFILIATIVE
(13.6)   (9.4)

4.6   3.8

2.8

IV. Rebellious   7.1   VII. Cooperative

V. Self-Effacing   VI. Docile

SUBMISSIVE
(9.9)

Director Baker

DOMINANT
(12.1)

II. Competitive   I. Managerial

III. Aggressive   VIII. Responsible

6.8   5.3

5.6   7.1

HOSTILE   AFFILIATIVE
(9.0)   (12.7)

3.4   5.6

1.6

IV. Rebellious   6.6   VII. Cooperative

V. Self-Effacing   VI. Docile

SUBMISSIVE
(8.2)

and one co-worker who is separated. Numbers of children range from none to two.

In terms of educational status, Joe is more like his subordinates than his peers and his boss. With the exception of one subordinate who has just a college education, staff members, like Joe, hold master's or other professional degrees. Most of Joe's peers as well as his boss, however, have doctoral degrees (Ph. D.'s or M. D.'s).

Hence Joe is in some ways in an insecure position. He has been in his organization for just one year. He is trying to make it in a new life outside the Church, and he has a lower education status than most of his peers and his boss.

In some ways Joe's newness is a strength. Co-workers describe him as having the vigor and flexibility of someone who is tackling a new challenge and is not yet settled in his ways. In accord with his male stereotype, Joe thinks categorically, in terms of the organization as a whole. He has a plan and goals for his clinic. Co-workers praise him for his "farsighted" goals, his "broad outlook" and his "good planning."

Furthermore, Joe is "energetic" and "aggressive" in the pursuit of his goals. He does not give up easily. Indeed, he "follows through" and has "moved the organization" in the short time that he has been its leader. Joe's intense efforts to assure the future of the organization and his willingness to fight the system create the impression that he is "genuinely concerned about the clinic and its people."

In addition to the tough and aggressive pursuit of organizational goals, Joe's planning process is creative. He is "imaginative" and "open to new things." New ideas come partly from Joe's expertise. He "knows the field well." Creativity is also fostered through attention to process. Being a "stickler for process" allows others' ideas to be brought out and incorporated into plans for the organization.

Joe's interpersonal strengths are clearly second to his organizational capabilities. Only one co-worker describes him as being "easy to get along with." Another vote of appreciation is for being "willing to give positive feedback."

Other comments concerning his interpersonal strengths are ambiguous. He is described as being "concerned about everyone," yet this means that he takes people "under his wing" (hence his extremely high dominant score on the style profile). Joe is likewise praised because he "tries to be thoroughly honest," but this co-worker adds "He doesn't always succeed." Joe's belief in process may exceed his ability to facilitate such sessions, or he may be over-using the processing motif in this setting. A conflict clearly exists between his high dominance and his attempt to run the organization through "processing" or participatory procedures.

This conflict is the major theme of the critical comments regarding Joe's leadership. Some co-workers are only aware of their confusion: "He is not clear in his communications." "He is inconsistent, surprises me with his moods."

Other co-workers are more explicit in describing the conflict: "Joe has a tendency to get too personal. He's unable to separate roles. He deals with staff as both therapist and administrator. This is threatening to the staff. The trust factor is off. He keeps people off balance. A good supervisor must be goal-oriented. [A staff member] should see that support is available; but privacy and space are needed."

Joe has violated the aloof male stereotype too much. This subordinate has eloquently described the wish and expectation that Joe remain in his task-oriented, administrator role, guiding the organization toward its goals from a more distant vantage point. The staff member is uncomfortable with a male leader's extension of the role into the personal, process-oriented mode.

Other critical comments focus on the extreme quality of some of Joe's male attributes. In his energetic and aggressive pursuit of organizational goals, he can be "a perfectionist," "uptight and pressured." Sometimes he "moves too fast for everyone to keep up." He "allows himself to take on more burden than he should." This overload of work makes Joe "impatient" with others who cannot keep up.

Another unfortunate consequence of Joe's fast paced style is a quality that relates to his high "hostile" score on the style profile. He "jumps to conclusions and acts on incomplete information." "He is overhasty in placing blame." "He blows up quickly." He has been known to "explode with anger." Joe's displays of emotion are very different from the business-like, aloof male leader stereotype.

Even with all of his difficulties as a leader, Joe's Role Assumption score ranks a moderate fourth among the twelve leaders of the study. The highest items support the high dominant score of Joe's style profile and his strong performance of the duties as a strategic planner for his organization: #10) "He is easily recognized as the leader of the group." The next highest items follow this dominant theme: #5) "He is (never) the leader of the group in name only," and #9) "He overcomes attempts to challenge his leadership."

The lowest items on Joe's Role Assumption Subscale relate to the critical comments concerning his less than successful use of process: #4 "He (never) lets some members take advantage of him." Joe describes staff meetings as a place where he opens himself to criticism from his staff and then often gets more than he can handle. In the eyes of co-workers, too, he is taken advantage of.

The next lowest item of the Role Assumption Subscale relates to his unsatisfactory decision-making style: #2) "He (never) fails to take necessary action." If Joe jumps to conclusions and acts on insufficient information as co-workers report, then it follows logically that he would sometimes fail to take necessary action.

Joe's rank is relatively lower on the Initiating Structure Subscale than on the Role Assumption Subscale. (He ranks sixth out of seven rankings.) His lowest item on this subscale underlines the professional nature of the work that his people are doing: #8) "He schedules work to be done." The next lowest item concurs with the confusion expressed by his staff and co-workers: #1) "He lets group members know what is expected of them"

Joe's dominant and authoritarian qualities are brought out clearly in the three highest items of the Initiating Structure Subscale: #2) "He encourages the use of uniform procedures," #5) "He decides what shall be done and how it shall be done," and #10) "He asks that group members follow standard rules and regulations."

Susan Baker, Clinic Director

Although younger than her male counterpart, at age thirty-one Susan Baker is like Joe Ryan in several ways. She too has been in her current position for just one year. She too has an educational background at the master's degree level. She too has never been married and has come to this position from her life in the Church.

Susan's work group is more female than Joe's, although both clinics serve clients of either sex. With the exception of one male subordinate, all of Susan's co-workers who participated in the study are women. Susan is in the unusual position of having subordinates who are older than herself (ages thirty-six, forty, and forty-six) and a boss who is two years her junior.

In terms of seniority, Susan's one year of tenure is not unusual. The number of years in the organization ranges from one to six for co-workers with an average of three years. Susan's boss has been in the organization for three years.

Susan is like her peers in terms of educational background. All of her peers as well as her boss, like Susan, hold master's degrees. Susan's subordinates, on the other hand, are all somewhat less highly educated. Two subordinates are college graduates and one has attended some college courses but has not graduated.

Lifestyles of co-workers are varied in terms of marital status, numbers of children and the extent to which spouses work outside the home. One peer, like Susan, has never been married, four co-workers currently are married, one subordinate is separated from her husband, and one peer is widowed. All of the subordinates who participated in the study have children as well as one of the peers. The numbers of children range from two to seven.

Much of the extremely strong praise for this "super human being," this "fine administrator," is related to her affiliative score on the style profile. (Although higher than Joe Ryan's, her male counterpart, Susan's score ranked a very moderate ninth among the twelve leaders of the study.) Her co-workers are nearly unanimous in their praise of her supervisory style, of her sensitivity in keeping just the right distance from subordinates.

Some of her supervisory "savvy" applies to everyone on the staff. She creates an "atmosphere that is ideal to work in." Part of what is ideal about the atmosphere in Susan's office is the openness of lines of communication. She herself "keeps an open mind with subordinates." She is receptive to ideas from subordinates. She is even willing to listen, change, risk and try new things. She has "warmth and empathy with her staff."

Susan can speak as well as listen. She is described as being bold and assertive in staff meetings—yet not excessively or inappropriately so. "Her manner of presentation gets the point across quickly." "She is a risk-taker: brings things up in meetings (after weighing the consequences) where someone else might not." "She is honest with herself and others, doesn't keep her mouth closed. She has a diplomatic way of dealing with problems that can become large."

Susan also is praised for her ability to speak up to those in positions of higher authority. She is described as a good "middle manager who has a diplomatic way of dealing with upper management to get what she wants for her subordinates." She is seen as having "courage in confronting authority figures."

The quality which is most frequently spoken of as what makes Susan a special kind of leader is the way she relates to subordinates as individuals. She creates a "close and cohesive" work group while acknowledging individual differences. She recognizes differences in ideas; "She is supportive of ideas of the less powerful, and gives recognition to their ideas." Susan also recognizes differences in work styles: "She is sensitive to needs. Self-starters don't need too much supervision and she lets us go with our own natural instincts."

Susan can "push when necessary," however, and she "follows through even if some responsibility is delegated." "She allows one to set their own pace within reason." Like Paul Meyer, administrator for the school district, Susan is viewed as a leader who carves out an area of freedom within the bureaucracy for her subordinates and thereby protects and encourages each staff member's growth and development.

Secondary in importance to her interpersonal strengths, Susan has other leadership attributes. She has expertise, "knowledge of psychodynamics," and "interviewing skills." She also has organizational skills, "plans her time well," "works [effectively] even under difficult conditions."

Furthermore, Susan is "enthusiastic about her work." Doing a good job is important to her. Yet her motives are "pure." She is not seen as being too ambitious or self-serving. On the contrary, Susan has "character."

What are Susan's weaknesses as a leader? Co-workers cite occasional instances where Susan loses control. Her close involvement with her staff means that sometimes she gets "really involved in a situation," not maintaining enough distance to have objectivity. "She couldn't say 'I'm not going to get upset and mean it.'" "She tends to personalize things."

The one male subordinate of Susan's staff who participated in the study describes the following incident to illustrate this point: In accord with office procedures, Dave supplied Susan with the data she required for reviewing her employees' performance.   Before she had a chance to consider the material, Susan left for vacation.

During her absence Dave noticed that other people were using Susan's office. He became concerned that the confidential material for his performance review was accessible to whomever was in the office. Subsequently Dave retrieved the file from his boss' office.

Upon her return, Susan noticed the missing file and called Dave to her office. She "reacted very strongly" and suggested that Dave must be "very angry." Dave maintains that the matter was finished business to him, that he was not angry, and that, furthermore, he did not want to deal with the incident as an emotional issue. He felt that Susan should have been more business-like.

Other criticisms of Susan's leadership relate to her willingness to take risks with new ideas. One consequence of this strategy is that she "changed directions a number of times." Sometimes the number was so great that she created confusion.

Her energy and intelligence leads her to occasionally "take on too much, over-extend herself." In her enthusiasm for her work she "gets frustrated" and is not tolerant of slowness or "stupidity" in others. In her haste, decision-making may also suffer. She does not always "think things through."

On the Role Assumption Subscale, Susan ranks first along with Carol Victor (see Chapter Two). For this highly praised leader, first place comes as no surprise. The highest items simply underline Susan's legitimation as a leader. Item #5 received the highest possible score: "She is (never) the leader of the group in name only." The next highest item is #10) "She is easily recognized as the leader of the group."

The lowest item on Susan's Role Assumption Subscale describer her non-authoritarian style of leadership: #9) "She overcomes attempts to challenge her leadership." In her empathy and acceptance of suggestions for change from subordinates she is seen as not defending herself against challenges to her authority.

The value placed on this descriptive statement is not clear. While this was Susan's lowest item, it was one of Joe Ryan's highest. Joe is criticized for being too authoritarian and appears to be extremely dominant in his style profile. Susan, on the other hand, is praised for her ability to listen and entertain ideas from subordinates as well as her ability to delegate responsibility and allow staff to do things in their own individual ways.

Another interesting point in comparing the Role Assumption Scales of Susan and Joe is that Susan's score was higher on seven of the ten items of the scale. The three items where Joe's score exceeded Susan's underline Joe's relatively authoritarian style: #8) "He/she takes full charge when emergencies arise," #9) "He/she overcomes attempts to challenge his/her leadership." #10) "He/she is easily recognized as the leader of the group."

Susan's overall score on the Initiating Structure Subscale was also higher than Joe's (for Susan: $\overline{X}$ = 4.2; for Joe: $\overline{X}$ = 4.0). Susan ranked fourth and Joe sixth out of seven rankings. Susan's superior communication skills are brought out in the three most discrepant items in which she scored higher than Joe: #1) "She lets group members know what is expected of them." (This item was Joe's lowest and Susan's highest.) #4) "She makes her attitudes clear to the group," and #7) "She makes sure that her part in the group is understood by group members."

Finally, support for the image of Joe as the more authoritarian of this pair of leaders comes from the leaders' scores on item #5) "He/she decides what shall be done and how it shall be done." This was Susan's lowest item and Joe Ryan's highest.

CRIMINAL JUSTICE AGENCY

Ron Smith and Anna Ferrari are directors of social service agencies that deal with the criminal justice system. The agencies provide counseling and other support services to people convicted of crimes. Like Susan Baker and Joe Ryan, Ron and Anna are responsible for all aspects of the operation of their respective agencies. These duties include seeking out funding sources for the agencies, hiring, firing and supervising a staff of counselors who work directly with the clients, and relating to the board of directors as well as to other governmental, judicial, and social service agencies.

With this pair of leaders, sex stereotypes are poor predictors of style profiles. Director Smith, the more affiliative, more submissive and less dominant leader is the man. Director Ferrari, the more dominant, less affiliative, and less submissive leader is the woman. The greatest difference in scores, however, is seen in the hostility dimension with Anna Ferrari having the higher score. Anna's profile is an example of the iron maiden stereotype, dominant and hostile.

Ron Smith, Agency Director

Ron Smith is a fifty-five year old white administrator. He has been in his current position for five years. Ron's educational background includes a master's degree.

As is appropriate for an agency which serves male prisoners, most of Ron's co-workers are men. Of the participants in the leadership study, all of the peers and two out of three of the subordinates are men. One of Ron's subordinates and one of his bosses, a member of his board of Directors, are women.

Ron's five years of seniority make him, relatively speaking, a newcomer to the agency. All of Ron's subordinates have been in the organization longer than himself (eight, nine and twenty-six years). Two (out of three) of Ron's peers have been directing their respective agencies for twenty years or more.

Ron's co-workers are mixed in terms of race (three of the participants are black and four are white). In terms of marital and family status, however, they are completely homogeneous. All participants, including Ron, are married and all have children.

Ron's educational background is consistent with co-workers'. All of his peers, like Ron, have master's degrees. A master's degree is also the usual background of subordinates, although one employee is unusual in having a doctoral degree. However, since appointment to the board of directors is based on other criteria, the board member who participated in the study has just a high school education.

Ron is generally recognized as a leader in his field, as having "great leadership ability." His staff cite his connections and skill in carrying out the political activities of his position as a major strength of their leader. One staff member states that he has "great experience" and is "internationally known among social reform agencies." Another staff member notes that he has "good skills appearing before

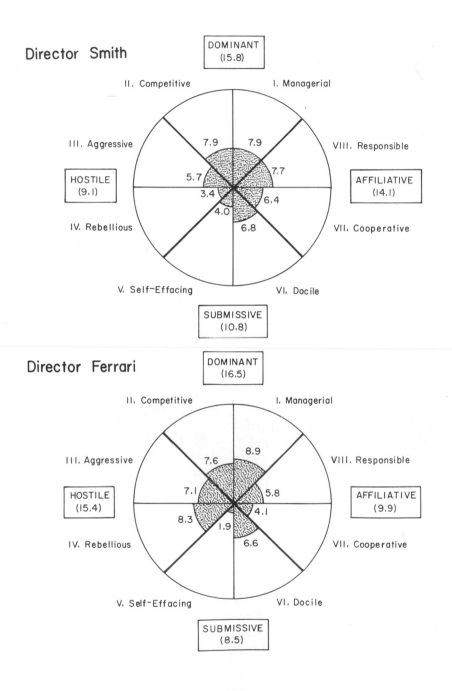

FIGURE 4-2

Criminal Justice Agency

Director Smith

DOMINANT (15.8)

II. Competitive   I. Managerial

III. Aggressive   VIII. Responsible

7.9   7.9

5.7   7.7

HOSTILE (9.1)   AFFILIATIVE (14.1)

3.4   6.4

4.0

IV. Rebellious   6.8   VII. Cooperative

V. Self-Effacing   VI. Docile

SUBMISSIVE (10.8)

Director Ferrari

DOMINANT (16.5)

II. Competitive   I. Managerial

III. Aggressive   VIII. Responsible

7.6   8.9

7.1   5.8

HOSTILE (15.4)   AFFILIATIVE (9.9)

8.3   4.1

1.9

IV. Rebellious   6.6   VII. Cooperative

V. Self-Effacing   VI. Docile

SUBMISSIVE (8.5)

legislative committees and relating this agency to the legislature."

One of the happy consequences of Ron's political clout is that he has been able to improve the status and financial standing of the agency. He has increased the number of sponsors of the organization. Ron is viewed as being very "conscientious" in the application of his leadership abilities to the development of this agency.

Like his male stereotype, Ron is "circumspect." He maintains enough of a distance from his staff that he can operate from a broad, organizational viewpoint. "He thinks things out well beforehand, then sticks to his guns after setting the rules." Ron appears to be consistent and well organized.

Nonetheless, Ron has "compassion." He is "accessible to staff members," maintaining an "open door." He even "takes advice well" from subordinates. While maintaining a business-like posture, Ron is seen as caring about staff members as people.

Ron's circumspection can be extreme, however. He sometimes "does not appear to respond as quickly as others might think he should." He appears to be "dragging his feet." This weakness in Ron's leadership can be described as not measuring up to the active and aggressive male stereotype.

One of Ron's staff criticizes him for being excessively political. Ron is seen as being "unwilling to make enemies" and as being directed solely by "goals imposed from the outside," e.g., the Board of Directors. In this view he lacks a "personal agenda" that would energize the agency and provide a sense of having a mission.

Another related criticism is that he "tries to do too much at one time." "He could do better at delegating authority." When the work load becomes too great "business [of the organization] causes a breakdown in communication [between Ron and the staff.]"

Ron's Role Assumption score ranks a moderate sixth among the twelve leaders of the study. The highest scoring items support the comments concerning his recognition as a leader in his field. The highest item is #5) "He is (never) the leader of the group in name only." The next highest items are #8) "He takes full charge when emergencies arise," and #10) "He is easily recognized as the leader of the group."

Ron's lowest item on this scale relates to the comments concerning his occasional slowness in decision-making: #2) "He (never) fails to take necessary action." Ron had recently fired a staff member at the time the study was conducted in his organization. There was general criticism among the staff that the decision was long overdue and that Ron had "dragged his feet" in this instance.

Ron received one of the lower scores among the twelve leaders on the Initiating Structure Subscale. His "compassionate" leadership is brought out in the highest and lowest scoring items. The lowest items underline the non-authoritarian nature of Ron's leadership: #2) "He encourages the use of uniform procedures." #5) "He decides what shall be done and how it shall be done," and #8) "He schedules work to be done." The highest item relates to his "open door" and the open lines of communication between himself and his staff: #7) "He makes sure that his part in the group is understood by group members."

Anna Ferrari, Agency Director

Anna is the same age as her male counterpart, Ron Smith. She is fifty-four. She is the most senior member of her agency, having worked there for nine years. Also, like Ron, her educational background includes a master's degree.

All of Anna's co-workers who participated in the study are women. One is black and the rest are white. A majority of these women are divorced or separated or remarried after divorce. Only one subordinate and one peer are married for the first time. Numbers of children range from none to three.

Anna's co-workers are slightly less educated than Ron's. Although the majority of co-workers, like Anna, hold master's degrees, one subordinate has just had some college work, and one peer as well as the board member who participated in the study are college graduates.

Similar to the reaction from Ron's staff, when asked to describe Anna's strengths as a leader, people focus first on her role as developer of the Agency. Anna's staff members are favorably impressed with their leader's hard work and dedication to the mission of the organization: "She did a hell of a job developing the program and maintaining the program for seven years. That says a lot for her as an individual." "She's very dedicated, consistently hard-working. It made me willing to work hard for the organization." She is unanimously viewed as being "very sincere about her work."

Anna's dedication to her work is evident in her manner of conducting staff meetings. One observer describes her: "She was work oriented and her contact with me was business oriented." This staff member is pleased that her female supervisor is so able to remain business-like in staff meetings.

In addition to being hard-working, Anna is viewed as having the intelligence and organizational skills required for leadership. One staff member describes her as "bright." Another notes that she is "well organized and articulate" and is capable of being "clear about what she wants."

Compassion, humanism, interpersonal skills are noticeably missing from the comments concerning Anna's strengths as a leader. One remark that she is "perceptive about people" is the only positive statement about her relationships with her co-workers. The comment is more a reiteration of her intelligence than a description of consideration.

On the other hand, Anna's high hostility score on the style profile is explained by co-workers' comments on her weaknesses as a leader. These comments unanimously describe some aspect of her "lack of ability to relate well to co-workers and subordinates." For all her intelligence, she does not transfer her perceptiveness about people into effective relations: "She's so knowledgeable about people, but she treats them so badly. She loses their respect." The same comment comes in different words from another co-worker: "People respect her for her knowledge but don't like her. This hinders what she gets from her workers."

One reason that staff members find Anna so difficult to relate to is that "her leadership is erratic." In another's words, "she's a conflicting, contradictory type of person." Her supervision shifts from a position which "gives staff leeway for their own work and leadership," to a position where "she can oversee your actions in a demeaning way, questioning people's judgement," or being "very nitpicky." The consensus is that "she gets better results when she leaves people alone [to work] on their own."

Although these criticisms are so pervasive among Anna's staff members, she is viewed as being unreceptive to criticism or feedback from her subordinates. She has the stereotypically feminine flaw of overpersonalizing work issues. She has a "tendency to confuse the organization with herself personally which makes criticism difficult. She sees it as criticism of herself."

One staff member notes that Anna is so sensitive to criticism that she exacts an extreme form of loyalty from her employees. She perceives other agencies (with which she competes for funding) as enemies. The staff member describes Anna's attitude as an "us against the world mentality." Consequently, any comment that is favorable to another agency is viewed as disloyal and evokes an angry response from Director Ferrari.

Anna ranks eighth among the twelve leaders on the Role Assumption Subscale. Her close domination of subordinates' work and her poor ability to delegate responsibility are brought out in the two highest scoring items: #10) "She is easily recognized as the leader of the group," and #5) "She (never) is the leader of the group in name only." As the more authoritarian of the pair, Anna's score on this subscale is higher than Ron's.

On the other hand, the disrespect which staff members have for their leader is evident in the items which scored lowest on this subscale: #7) "She (never) lets some members have authority she should keep," and #4) "She (never) lets some members take advantage of her."

Like her male counterpart, Anna Ferrari ranks next to last on the Initiating Structure Subscale. The one-way communication system in Anna's office, i.e., from the top down, is brought out in the items which have the greatest discrepancy between Anna's and Ron's scores. On two items Anna's score is the higher: #4) "She/he makes her/his attitudes clear to the group," and #3) "She/he tries out her/his ideas in the group." In her dominating style, Anna makes certain that her way of doing things is dictated to the group.

Anna's inability to solicit or receive feedback from her staff is underlined by the one item which is scored lower on Anna's subscale than on Ron's: #7) "She/he makes sure that her/his part in the group is understood by group members." Making sure would require listening to staff members' comments concerning their leader. According to staff members' descriptions, Ron's listening skills exceed Anna's.

CONCLUSION

Confusion is the result of attempting to understand these social service leaders in terms of sex stereotypes. Aggressiveness, a traditionally male quality, in the form of promoting the political interests of the organization is considered a virtue for all four leaders regardless of gender. Listening ability and compassion, traditionally female qualities, are positively valued in one female and one male leader, Susan and Ron. A business-like manner which allows subordinates a comfortable amount of space and leeway to work in their own unique ways—a traditionally male attribute—is credited to both Ron and Susan.

On the negative side, the "motherly" style of supervising or over-supervising by dominating and intervening in subordinates' work is attributed to one male and one female leader, Joe and Anna. Excessive emotion and overpersonalizing work isues is also attributed to leaders regardless of gender, i.e., Susan, Joe, and Anna.

Reviewing the cases of these leaders individually, signs of the traditional stereotypes exist along with evidence of the demise of these stereotypes. Joe Ryan is praised for demonstrating the traditional manly virtues of thinking categorically of the organization as a whole, and of aggressively pursuing organizational goals. Also traditionally, he is criticized for deviating from the macho male image with displays of emotions, behavior which is not business-like and aloof.

Other strengths and weaknesses attributed to Joe Ryan do not fit a sex stereotype explanation. On one hand Joe is criticized for excessive dominance in the form of "taking people under his wing"—a traditionally feminine nurturing activity. On the other hand he is complimented on his creative and imaginative thinking and his concern for people —also traditionally feminine qualities.

Susan Baker, one of the top leaders of the study, is praised for both "feminine" and "masculine" traits. Concurring with female stereotypes, Susan is open with subordinates and sensitive to individual needs. Concurring with male stereotypes, Susan is bold and assertive with her staff as well as with higher authorities.

Susan's weaknesses are also mixed in terms of sex stereotypes. She is criticized for getting too emotionally involved in work issues—like a woman. She is also criticized for being too quick for subordinates and intolerant of slowness in others— like a man.

Ron Smith presents a similarly confused picture. His strengths are his political connections and his circumspection or business-like stance with subordinates. These qualities are traditionally male. However, Ron is also viewed as having the traditional female virtues of compassion and accessibility to staff members.

Ron's weakness as a leader is measured against the male stereotype. He is too nice, i.e., political. He is unwilling to offend people and be tough enough in the pursuit of organizational goals.

Finally, Anna Ferrari presents another leadership portrait, mixed in terms of sex stereotypes. Like a woman, she is criticized for being excessively "nitpicky" and over-bearing in her supervision of subordinates. Also like a woman, she is described as overpersonalizing work issues and therefore reacting emotionally to matters of organizational business. Anna's dominant and hostile style profile fits the iron maiden stereotype.

Other characteristics ascribed to Anna do not fit the negative images of female leaders. She is praised for the way she works, aggressively confronting political forces for the sake of developing her organization. She is viewed as being outspoken, bright and articulate.

The boundaries of role encapsulation are expanded for both men and women who lead in these social service organizations. Like the male educational leaders, the boundaries of the strong and tough male leader stereotype have expanded to accommodate softer qualities such as Ron's compassion, Joe's creativity. Unlike the female educational leaders, however, the boundaries of the sensitive and democratic stereotype of the female leader has expanded to accommodate some stronger and tougher qualities: Susan's assertive and outspoken leadership, Anna's articulateness and aggression in promoting the well-being of her organization.

Yet along with these new freedoms are new limits. Joe and Anna are censured by subordinates for their dominant and interfering supervision without regard for the gender of the boss. *The "liberation" of these organizations is such that men (and women) are not simply allowed the freedom to lead in a softer, less authoritarian style, they are expected to do so, and are censured if they do not.*

I once interviewed a very attractive young woman who worked as a supervisor in a large private corporation. She made the perceptive comment, "a woman has to be assertive because she can't get away with being aggressive." For Joe Ryan, Clinic Director, men too can no longer get away with being aggressive.

Joe Ryan and Anna Ferrari are two of the most troubled leaders of the study. By their own reports they are floundering and groping for a consistent leadership style. In the eyes of their staff members, they are seen as being contradictory, unpredictable, and therefore difficult to work for.

How might this confusion be explained? Part of the answer lies in the dual nature of the role of the administrator of the human service organization. The job of the executive is to be aggressive in the political arena outside the organization as an advocate for social reform and in the pursuit of funding sources. On the other hand, the administrator is to be compassionate toward clients that the agency serves and super-competent in the listening skills and sensitivity of the counselor or therapist. This dilemma is described by scholars of the human service organization (Hasenfeld and English, 1977; Kendall, 1978).

Another explanatory source is some recent research literature on sex roles which is based upon field studies. These field studies have generally failed to replicate the evidence of sex stereotypes which were found in earlier laboratory studies (Ezell, Odewan and Sherman, 1980; Osborn and Vicars, 1976; Shingledecker and Terborg, 1980). The reasoning of these researchers goes as follows: Sex stereotypes fill in where gaps about a female leader exist. It is important for a subordinate to know what to expect from the boss. Therefore stereotyped expectations about a female leader will exist in situations where information based on personal experience is missing. Such information would be missing in either an experimental situation, e.g., a study conducted with management students in a college classroom, or in a work setting where women in leadership roles are scarce or unknown. Therefore sex stereotypes and negative attitudes toward women as leaders are more prevalent among people who have never worked for one (Bowman, Worthy and Greyser, 1965).

In her comprehensive work on *The Psychology of Sex Differences* (1974, p. 353), Eleanor Maccoby backs up this notion that experience and familiarity dissipate at least one sex stereotype, the image of the always dominant male:

> "The dominance relations between the sexes are complex: in childhood, the sex segregation of play groups means that neither sex frequently attempts to dominate the other . . . Among adult mixed pairs or groups, formal leadership tends to go to males in the initial phase of interaction, but the direction of influence becomes more sex-equal the longer the relationship lasts with division of authority occurring along lines of individual competencies and division of labor."

Finally, Kurt Lewin's model of social change provides a satisfying explanation for the confusion created by the evidence which partly supports and partly does not support the notion that traditional sex stereotypes (of the strong, aggressive and aloof male leader, and the emotional and non-assertive female leader and the dominating "bitchy" female leader) still are providing standards against which leaders are assessed. The first step in the change process, "unfreezing" involves a "reduction in the strength of old values," a "disturbance of equilibrium," in short, confusion (Lewin, 1951). The old double standard: Women are perceived as incompetent until proven capable and men are perceived as capable until proven incompetent, is not fair, but it is clear. The emerging new standard is not so clearly defined. In this climate of social change the confusion is an optimistic sign, a sign that unfreezing of old values exists. Yet the discomfort of Anna's and Joe's "confusing, contradictory" leadership is easy to understand.

NOTES

1. Compare the 16 percent of social service agencies directed by women of the National Association of Social Workers survey to the results of a survey conducted by the public relations firm, Burson-Marsteller. In 1,300 businesses including banks, utilities, financial and insurance companies

women represented only one percent of top management and five to six percent of middle management (Fowler, 1977).

2. Average scores on the Women as Managers Scale (WAMS) for the employees of the three kinds of organizations were as follows: business, 116.2; education, 124.9; social service, 127.4. A higher score indicates more positive attitudes toward women in management. The scores represent a continuum with the business organizations having the least positive attitudes toward women managers, the social service organizations having the most positive attitudes and the educational organizations falling in between. The educational organizations are, however, more similar to the social service than the business organizations.

CHAPTER FIVE: MEN VIEW THEMSELVES AS LEADERS

> "He must be under great self-control in a
> situation where control is difficult.   If,
> therefore, he must know his men well, he
> must know himself still better.   He must
> know the passions in him that, unchecked,
> will destroy him as a leader, and he must
> know their sources in his personality.   For
> how can we control a force, the source of
> whose energy we do not know?   Self-
> knowledge is the first step to self-control."

George C. Homans, *The Human Group*

Joe Ryan, clinic director, asked me to provide him with
feedback on the results of the leadership study for his organization. In response, I wrote him the following letter:

Dear Joe Ryan:

I am beginning this report with a qualification. I prefer
to give feedback in person rather than by mail so that
misunderstandings may be clarified immediately. Nonetheless, I am sending you an analysis of two parts of the
questionnaires from yourself and your co-workers. One part
is a leadership style profile[1] and the other is part of a standardized leadership research questionnaire.[2]
For both instruments, I have included your self-
perceptions and a composite view of your leadership from the
perspectives of seven co-workers including subordinates,

peers and superiors. My purpose in doing so is to allow you to look at discrepancies between your self-perceptions and the perceptions of co-workers. Leaders that I have worked with on a consulting basis have found that examining such discrepancies is useful.

Before I begin the analysis of the questionnaires, however, I would like to remind you of your own description of your strengths and weaknesses, as a leader. I think that the questionnaires can best be understood in the context of your subjective comments. You pride yourself, first, on having sensitivity and awareness of both yourself and others. You describe yourself as an "open" person who has a "sense of my own abilities," a "sense of direction," and a "healthy self-concept." Furthermore, you are "sensitive to others' personal struggles."

As an organization man, you see your strength lying in your "willingness to risk." Because of this willingness you have "enhanced the creativity" of those who work for you. Furthermore, in fostering the development of your office, you are "able to overcome opposition."

Your weaknesses as a leader are related to your strengths. Your sensitivity to others causes you to occasionally "lose perspective, getting personally involved in personality conflicts and losing the wider picture." Your high goals lead you to occasionally have "expectations that are unrealistic for myself and for others." In your words, "This can be self-defeating."

Now, let's return to the questionnaires, and look first at the interpersonal style profile that you drew of yourself. You are primarily dominant and affiliative, operating by managing the work of others and personally bearing responsibility. Another major component of your style is being "docile." This quality comes from delegating authority, or practicing a form of participative management where the leadership is shared. A secondary but still significant element of your style is "aggressiveness."

Now looking at the profile that your co-workers drew: (see Chapter Four) In comparison to the profile that you drew of yourself, your co-workers see you as being more dominant and less affiliative. They also see you as less "docile," practicing a less participative form of management. The discrepancies are better understood when looking at the Role

Assumption and Initiating Structure Subscales of the leadership questionnaire.

You see yourself as letting others take away your leadership more often than your co-workers do. They see you as overcoming attempts to challenge your leadership more often than you do. You see yourself as being taken advantage of more often than they do. These results seem to be consistent with the style profiles which indicate that your co-workers see you as being more dominant and delegating authority less than you do.

To sum up, I shall make a guess which is based only on this information: my guess is that since you feel you often let others take away your leadership, seldom overcoming challenges, and that you occasionally let others take advantage of you, you may be doing some things to regain your leadership which are coming across to others as more dominating and hostile than you intend. Perhaps seeing in this feedback that your co-workers do indeed see you as being a powerful leader may change your own perceptions of how much authority you maintain. I hope that this report will be helpful to you. If all is not clear, please let me know. I would be happy to discuss it further with you.

Cordially,

Trudy Heller

This diagnosis of the interaction between the way Joe sees himself as a leader and the way co-workers see him, the mutual influence of one on the other provides a clear example of a role theory model of leadership in action. According to this model co-workers (subordinates, peers and superiors) have expectations of how the leader should behave. They communicate their expectations to the leader who is more or less sensitive to these expectations. The leader combines a reading of co-workers' expectations with self-imposed expectations and the resulting behavior is a compromise of these different and sometimes conflicting expectations.

In the case of Joe Ryan, the cycle goes as follows: co-workers at the alcohol clinic expect the person in Joe's position to be nonauthoritarian, delegating substantial amounts of responsibility, leaving staffers their own "space" in which to work. These expectations may be based upon traditions established by Joe's predecessor, or upon norms of the organization or the profession of mental health workers, or upon the individual histories of employees and their attitudes toward authority. Co-workers communicate these expectations to Joe, the director.

Joe, the other party in this process of role definition, receives from co-workers the expectation that he lead in a participative, non-authoritarian style. Considering these expectations to be legitimate and wanting to succeed in his new leadership position, Joe alters his naturally rather authoritarian style in the direction desired by co-workers. But still a discrepancy exists between Joe's behavior and co-workers' expectations. Hence Joe's compromised style of performing his role appears to be too authoritarian to meet the co-workers expectations and too non-authoritarian to meet Joe's expectations of himself.

Co-workers respond to Joe's behavior by increasing their efforts to influence him to change his style which appears to be dominating and authoritarian to them. Since Joe already feels that he has given up a substantial amount of authority, he responds by "bearing down" even harder—and so the cycle continues.

Presumably Joe and his co-workers will arrive at a negotiated and mutually influenced definition of his leadership role. Confronting Joe with the current discrepancies may facilitate this process.[3] According to the theory, the conflict caused by the discrepant expectations or images of Joe are dysfunctional in terms of personal stress (for everyone) and effectiveness (for Joe and the clinic) (Kahn, et al., 1964).

Other theories provide other reasons why it is important for a leader to have accurate self-perceptions. In his classic work, *The Human Group,* George Homans (1950) suggests that leaders must know themselves in order to have self-control, a prerequisite for controlling followers. Karl Weick (1978, p. 55) describes the importance of self-acceptance—a prerequisite for self-awareness—to a leader: " . . . deficiencies in self-acceptance have obvious costs in psychological pain . . . these deficiencies also have other less obvious costs because they erode the variety a leader has available to control and regulate the variety that confronts him." Weick's notion is that a leader acts as a medium, sensing complexities and variety in the environment, integrating and controlling the diversity for followers. The greater a leader's self-acceptance and the more accurate the self-perceptions, the richer are the leader's capabilities to serve as a medium.

Another theme in the literature on self-perception concerns sex differences and the notion that women have greater self-awareness and sensitivity to how others see them than men do. One source of this idea is the stereotyping of women as the sex which is "very aware of feelings of others" (Broverman, et al., 1972, p. 63). Another source is the theory that women have a greater inclination to self-reflect because every month their attention is turned inward to the emotional variations of the menstrual cycle (Bateson, 1972). A final explanation for women's greater self-awareness is the notion that they are the sensitive sex because they are "outsiders" to the mainstream of American society. The discipline of Women Studies can, for example, be viewed as the self-contemplation of the academic woman (Weskott, 1979).

Yet rarely, if ever, is the logic of these two themes extended to the assumption that women are better qualified for leadership because of their greater self-awareness. On the contrary, female self-awareness is viewed as excessive, uncontrolled and detrimental to successful leadership. In his discussion of the poor capacity for self-disclosure (one has to be self-aware in order to self-disclose) as a "lethal aspect of the male role," Jourard (1974, p. 24) states: "Studies of leadership show that the leaders of the most effective groups maintain an optimum 'distance' from their followers, avoiding the distraction thereby of overly intimate personal knowledge of the followers' immediate feelings and needs (Fiedler, 1957). But not all of a man's everyday life entails the instrumental role . . . Personal life calls both for insight and for empathy. If practice at spontaneous self-disclosure promotes insight and empathy, then perhaps we have here one of the mechanisms by which women become more adept at their 'expressive' role. Women trained toward motherhood and a comforting function, both engage in and receive more self-disclosure than men" (Jourard and Richman, 1963). Hence women's insightfulness and empathy has traditionally been used to exclude them from the executive suite in spite of theoretical evidence that insight and self-awareness are requisites of successful leadership.

Two sets of questions, then, become interesting in looking at the self-perceptions of the leaders in this study. One set of questions concerns the extent of the discrepancies between the leaders' own views of their leadership and the views of co-workers. Questions such as whether, compared to men, women see themselves more as others do can be addressed in examining these discrepancies. The other set of questions concerns the content of the discrepancies. Questions such as whether the leaders describe themselves more or less in accord with sex stereotypes can be discussed in considering the leaders' self-reports.

Organizational consultants have, for a long time, understood the value of feedback to leaders. Leaders have found that examining differences between the way they see themselves and the way others see them to be useful. The exploration of such discrepancies will be exploited as a research tool in this discussion of how men and women view themselves as leaders. To this end, I have imagined that each of Joe Ryan's eleven fellow leaders was a client in a consulting process rather than a subject of research.

A series of letters addressed to the would-be leaders-as-clients will systematically explore the similarities and contrasts between the leaders' views of themselves and the viewpoints of co-workers. Reports to the male leaders are contained in Chapter Five. The business leaders are addressed first: Dan Monroe, travel agency manager and Jim Stevens, project director of a large, private corporation. Following the businessmen are two male educational leaders: Paul Meyer, administrator for the school district and Herb Weiss, department chairman at the University. Completing the presentation of the male leaders, the other social service leader is addressed, Ron Smith, director of a criminal justice agency.

The six female leaders are then considered in Chapter Six. Comparisons between the men and women are drawn from this rich source of information. Trends and conclusions are discussed in terms of the questions suggested above, e.g., are the women more self-aware? Do the leaders subscribe to the sex stereotypes?

Dear Dan Monroe: (Travel Agency Manager)

I am writing to you at the travel agency to report on the results of the leadership study. Specifically, I am going to respond to your request for information on differences between the way you describe yourself as a manager and the way co-workers describe you. You may recall that the co-workers included in the study are your boss, the owner of the travel agency, your peer, Manager Grant, and a selected sample of your staff of travel agents. I shall begin with your description of your strengths and weaknesses as a leader, then move on to considering the questionnaires.

The strengths which you ascribe to your leadership are what I call "task-oriented" rather than "people-oriented." These terms simply mean that you describe characteristically strong ways of doing your work rather than focusing on relations with your staff. You state that you are "dependable" in the performance of your job, and that you "plan and schedule" the work that you do through your ability to "convey ideas well."

Unlike your strengths, the weakness you ascribe to yourself is "people-oriented." You state that you are "not forceful enough" in dealing with co-workers. I'm sure you are wondering whether co-workers agree with these assessments of your strengths and weaknesses.

First, let's look at the two style profiles, one that represents your self-description and the other that represents co-workers' descriptions of your interpersonal style. On the profile that you drew of yourself, you are primarily affiliative and secondarily submissive. On your co-workers' profile these two dimenstions are reversed: you are primarily submissive and secondarily affiliative (see Chapter Two).

A look at the Role Assumption and Initiating Structure Subscales points out specific areas in which your co-workers view you as more submissive. The items which are most discrepant on the Role Assumption Scale are: #9) "He overcomes attempts to challenge his leadership," and #10) "He is easily recognized as the leader of the group." On both of these descriptions, you see yourself as being more forceful than do your co-workers.

The most discrepant items on the Initiating Structure Subscale, likewise, point out specific areas in which you see yourself as more assertive than do your co-workers. On all three of the most discrepant items your self-ratings are higher than co-workers: You indicate that you "try out ideas in the group," "schedule work to be done" and "maintain definite standards of performance" more often than co-workers indicate you do. The items are very similar to the leadership strengths you reported in your interview: planning, scheduling and conveying ideas well.

Finally, let me add to this information some of the comments that your co-workers made concerning your strengths and weaknesses as a leader. On the positive side, I think that co-workers value your affiliative nature and your nonauthoritarian style more than you think. Comments such as "nice guy," "easy to work for," "not too demanding," express a positive valuing of your not too dominant style. I think that co-workers would also agree with your description of yourself as being "dependable." In their words you are "honest," "loyal" and "businesslike."

As for the weaknesses of our leadership, I think that both you and your co-workers would agree that your management could be improved by adding a measure of assertiveness to the basically sound relationships that you have developed. The discrepancy between your view and your co-workers' viewpoint seems to be a matter of degree. You see your tendency to be "not forceful enough" as being less extensive than do co-workers. In the eyes of your co-workers this is a bigger problem than it is to you.

To summarize, I shall describe your situation in terms of a theoretical framework that we have discussed, role theory. Co-workers have certain expectations of you as a leader. Specifically, they expect you to be somewhat more dominant and forceful than you are. You understand and are sensitive to these expectations. You allow them to influence your behavior, and therefore assert yourself in areas in which you are most comfortable, e.g., scheduling and planning work. Co-workers still see you as lacking forcefulness, however, because they are focused on other aspects of your behavior, e.g., your interaction with your boss. Their perceptions of you in this critical area carry over to the other, stronger aspects of your leadership.

If you feel this material may need further clarification, please call with your questions and comments.

Cordially,

Trudy Heller

Dear Jim Stevens: (Project Director, large private corporation)

You and I have spent several hours in your office at corporate headquarters discussing the usefulness of feedback to leaders. For the sake of putting this theory into practice, I am sending you this report describing the differences beween the way you view yourself as project director and the way co-workers (subordinates, peers, and superiors) view your leadership. I trust that you will find it useful.

I shall begin by comparinq the two interpersonal style profiles, one which represents your self-perceptions, and one which represents your co-workers' viewpoint. You may recall that the profiles are organized around two dimensions, dominant-submissive and hostile-affiliative. Hence there are four major style qualities represented. On three of these characteristics your profile differs considerably from the profile that co-workers drew. You see yourself as being less affiliative, less hostile and more submissive than do your co-workers. On the dominant factor, perceptions are about the same.

Consistent with this congruence in perceptions of your dominance is the fact that the way you rated yourself on the Role Assumption Subscale is nearly identical to the way co-workers rated you. The only item that shows any remarkable difference is #5) "He is the leader of the group in name only." You report that this item is true more often than co-workers do. You state that this is "occasionally" the case, whereas co-workers think that you are "seldom" the leader of the group in name only. I suspect that this item may be related to the matrix structure of your organization and the fact that staff members have other home bases and other bosses— hence the feeling that you are the leader of the group in name only without the kind of legitimate authority backing you up that a boss in a traditional hierarchical organization would have.

The Initiating Structure Subscale provides some information that helps to explain the discrepancies between your self-perceptions and the perceptions of co-workers on the other dimensions of the style profile, the affiliative, submissive, and hostile dimensions. On two items of this scale, the discrepancy is such that you view yourself as providing less structure than co-workers indicate you do. On the most discrepant item you indicate that you "seldom decide what shall be done and how it shall be done," whereas co-workers think that you "often" provide this kind of structure. Similarly, on another item of this scale, you indicate that you "occasionally assign group members to particular tasks." From co-workers' viewpoint, however, you "often" make such assignments.

On another item of the Initiating Structure Scale, however, the discrepancy is in the other direction. Co-workers see you as providing less structure than you do. They report that you "occasionally" "ask that group members follow standard rules and regulations." You report that you "often" make such requests.

I think that these results are best understood, however, in the context of the comments made by yourself and your co-workers when asked to describe your strengths and weaknesses as a leader. To this end let me remind you of your own remarks. Your description of the interpersonal aspects of your leadership might be summarized by the term, "laid back." You state that your strengths lie in your ability to listen to subordinates with a "flexible and open attitude," "providing a lot of latitude for people" in order to "build their confidence." You also mention a motivator that works: "trying to explain [to subordinates] what effect their jobs have on other departments." The one weakness you attribute to your leadership is "not [being] a really dynamic type of individual, not trying to build an empire."

Do co-workers' reports of your strengths and weaknesses concur with your own? Co-workers generally agree with your description of your strengths. They too see you as being "open to new ideas," willing to try something new if it "sounds good." They also agree that you are "good at developing people" by encouraging them to do things on their own. Furthermore, co-workers view you as being "easy to get along with" and "an extremely decent human being."

As for the weaknesses of your leadership, co-workers agree that you are sometimes "not dynamic," sometimes show "a tendency toward indecision," sometimes "tend to be over-cautious." The other weakness that co-workers describe is an inconsistency in your strong behaviors. They cite occasions when you "become terribly hard on the people who work for you," losing your usual inclination to give people leeway. They also cite occasions when you lose your usual openness and become "a little bit too touchy" when people disagree with you.

To sum up, I shall try to put these pieces of information together into a coherent (and very hypothetical) model of how you and your co-workers interact. Your basic style is to be open, flexible and to give subordinates a fair amount of leeway. From your viewpoint this is a "laid back" or "submissive" style. To co-workers this style is more affiliative because it creates the impression that you are a humane leader. (Hence the discrepancy on the submissive dimension and the affiliative dimension.) On the other hand, you are not entirely consistent in this style, and in your weaker moments you appear to co-workers to be hostile, not allowing them the leeway they have come to expect, becoming "touchy" rather than "open" to critical comments. (Hence the discrepancy in the hostility dimension.)

Perhaps considering this new perspective on your style will be helpful to you. If you would like any further information, please let me know.

Sincerely yours,

Trudy Heller

Dear Paul Meyer: (Administrator for a School District)

As an educator and an administrator, I know that you are familiar with the value of self-confrontation as a learning technique. For the sake of such learning I am writing to you at the school district to report on both your self-perceptions and on perceptions of your performance as administrator provided by co-workers. I trust that you will find this report educational.

Let me begin by reminding you of the standards you set for yourself in describing your strengths as a leader. You state that you are primarily people-oriented, that you "care about people" while "recognizing the goals of the organization." You elaborate on your humanistic qualities. "People respond to my direction. I think I can protect creative people in the bureaucratic system while I take some of the heat. I can delegate without second-guessing."

Measured against this humanistic standard, you see your weaknesses as those "times in my work when, to get things done, I am too product-oriented. I tend to accept more for my operation than is good. The extra activity strains communication."

Consistent with these subjective descriptors of your leadership style is the interpersonal style profile which represents your self-perceptions. The highest dimension on your profile is the affiliative. The profile that represents co-workers' conception of your leadership is similar to your own.

Discrepancies between your view and that of your co-workers do appear, however, on the Role Assumption and Initiating Structure Subscales. Here you see yourself as being less directive than do your co-workers. Co-workers describe you as having more of those production-oriented qualities that you called weaknesses, such as encouraging the use of uniform procedures, scheduling work to be done and asking that group members follow standard rules and regulations. Co-workers also think that you are more likely to take full charge in emergencies and less likely to be the leader of the group in name only.

The value which co-workers put on these production-oriented activities may not be the same negative value which you attach to them, however. Co-workers comments indicate that they see you as meeting your goal of "translating the goals of the organization" into human terms. They cite as strengths of your leadership such production-oriented qualities as being "hard working," "well-organized," "resourceful" and "prepared." There are no comments indicating that workloads or emphasis on production is excessive.

Hence the discrepancy which I see between your own view and co-workers' view of your leadership is one of both content and values. Compared to yourself, co-workers see you as providing more structure and being more production-oriented. Furthermore, co-workers view these qualities as strengths—contrary to your own values. Perhaps some value reclassification is in order.

I hope that this report reaches you in one of your less busy times.

      Cordially,

      Trudy Heller

Dear Professor Herb Weiss: (Department Chairman at a university)

The results of the leadership study are finally in, and I am writing to report to you as promised. I know that you are familiar with the theory which asserts that the leader is the one who knows the most about the group in which he works. Based on this theoretical assumption, I have phrased this report in terms of discrepancies between the way you see yourself as department chairman and the way others (your faculty members, fellow department heads, and your boss, the dean) view your leadership.

Let me begin, therefore, by reminding you of the way you describe yourself, your strengths and weaknesses as a leader. In recounting both the pluses and minuses of your chairmanship, you focus on the interpersonal aspect of the leader's job: "I think that my strengths lie primarily in my sensitivity to people and understanding their situations."

The weakness of your leadership is described as an excess of that same quality. You state that your greatest weakness is "leniency." In your sensitivity and understanding of others it is not difficult to imagine you losing objectivity with your faculty (subordinates) to a point where leniency becomes a weakness.

In general co-workers tend to agree with your self-reported strengths and weaknesses. Your sensitivity and understanding is reiterated in such comments as,
"He is very personable, gets along well with his staff" and "I like him." Your so-called "leniency" is reported by co-workers as a lack of "fight" in dealing with the "higher authorities" in your university. Hence they emphasize your lack of combativeness in another area outside your department.

The Role Assumption and Initiating Structure Subscales as well as the interpersonal style profiles similarly reflect this trend: common views of the nature or quality of your

strengths and weaknesses as a leader, but differences in the
extensiveness of them. On both the Role Assumption and
Initiating Structure Subscales, your self-rating is lower than
the average rating of co-workers. On the Role Assumption
Subscale, however, differences are much greater than on the
Initiating Structure Subscale. You rate yourself lower than
the others on every item of this scale. Compared to your co-
workers' ratings on the most discrepant items you describe
yourself backing down more often, as being more hesitant
about taking initiative in the group, as more often being the
leader of the group in name only, as more often letting work
group members take advantage of you and take away your
leadership in the group.

These items are especially striking in contrast with a
series of comments made by your co-workers concerning your
strengths as a leader. The comments focus on your manner
of conducting departmental meetings. There is general
consensus that you "handle yourself very well." More significantly, your ability to "keep things organized" and "do the
leadership job" without being "authoritarian" is where your
strength lies in the eyes of co-workers. In sum, although co-
workers see you as being much more forceful and assertive
and strong in your leadership role, they do not see you as
being excessively so. You remain appropriately non-
authoritarian in their eyes.

This same discrepancy is apparent on the style profiles.
On the profile which represents co-workers' viewpoints, you
are primarily affiliative and secondarily submissive. A
similar pattern appears on the profile which represents your
self-perception: your interpersonal style appears primarily
affiliative and secondarily submissive. Yet there is a
substantial difference in the extent to which these qualities
exist in yours and on co-workers' profiles. On your own
profile you are extremely affiliative and considerably more
submissive than on the profile that co-workers drew.

In sum, you may be heartened by this report to learn that
your co-workers see you as having more force and legitimacy
as a leader than you see in yourself. Furthermore co-workers
do not fault you for these aspects of your "strength." They
still see you as a non-authoritarian leader—a point which
may be a source of pride to you. While they share your perception of yourself as being too "lenient" with higher author

ities and peers, they view you as exercising considerable, but not objectionable, strength within your own department.

If all of this report is not clear, let me know so that we might discuss the material further.

Cordially,

Trudy Heller

Dear Ron Smith: (Director of a Criminal Justice Agency)

I am writing to provide you with the feedback you requested on the information gathered from your criminal justice agency during the leadership study. In sending this report to you I am reminded of a comment you made during your interview. We were talking about the aftermath of the recent firing of one of your staff members and your uneasy feelings about the incident. You expressed the wish to know what others thought of your action: "The office should not be a gossip ground, but I wish I knew how others felt about my firing someone." I trust that this report will be a source of useful information to you as director of the agency.

Let me begin by reminding you of the strengths that you attributed to your leadership in your interview. You mentioned one task-oriented strength, being able to "organize things well," and two people-oriented strengths, being capable of "dealing with staffers and gaining their respect," and having an ability to "handle interpersonal conflict" when you are not personally involved.

On the negative side, you attribute the following weaknesses to your leadership. You state that you "do not like confrontation situations" when you are personally involved. A consequence of this avoidance of conflict is that you "tend to let things go until I have to act." You repeated this consequence using different words: "I have not been decisive sometimes when I should have nipped things in the bud."

This same issue which you focus on in discussing your weaknesses as a leader is evident in the information provided by the Role Assumption and Initiating Structure Scales as well as the interpersonal style profiles. Let's begin by examining the Role Assumption Scale. Here, in comparison to co-workers you generally describe yourself as being more laid back ("indecisive," "slow to act") in your leadership. On three of the most discrepant items, you indicate that you assert your leadership less often than do your co-workers, i.e., in the areas of letting other persons take away your leadership of the group, letting some members take advantage of you, and backing down when you ought to stand firm. On the other hand, you indicate that you overcome attempts to challenge your leadership more often than others do.

The same "mixed" pattern appears on the Initiating Structure Scale. On the two most discrepant items you indicate that you are more directive in terms of encouraging the use of uniform procedures and trying out your ideas in your work group. Yet on two other remarkably discrepant items, co-workers view you as more directive than you view yourself in terms of making your attitudes clear to the group, and scheduling work to be done.

Comparing the self-scored style profile with the profile that co-workers drew adds to the information provided by these scales. Here co-workers view you as having a balanced repertoire of interpersonal behaviors, especially being strong in the dominant and affiliative modes, and leading through managerial and responsible behaviors. The profile which you draw of yourself differs in that the emphasis is on the hostile and dominant dimensions. You describe yourself as being considerably more hostile than do your co-workers.

I suspect that this high hostility score relates to the incident alluded to in your interview. I'm referring to the recent firing of one of your staff members. According to your account of the incident, you had been too "nice" for too long, then, when the confrontation and firing finally occurred, it was done harshly and abruptly. I suspect that this critical incident is not atypical. It serves to explain both the high hostility score which you attribute to yourself at this particular time, as well as the mixed results on the Role Assumption and Initiating Structure Scales where you see yourself as being sometimes more assertive, directive or decisive (to use your term) and sometimes less.

One final point which I neglected to mention earlier is that co-workers' descriptions of your strengths indicate that they would strongly agree with the strengths you ascribe to yourself. In addition, they mention that you are a "good organizer." In terms of relating to your staff, they too think that you have won their respect. In their words you are "accessible" and "compassionate."

Although this report is not as well organized as I would like, I trust that it will make sense to you.

Cordially,

Trudy Heller

SUMMARY

To what extent are these men haunted by the stereotype of the male leader,—the tough, aggressive and business-like male image? For the business leaders, Dan Monroe and Jim Stevens, the spectre is most clearly in force. Both Dan and his co-workers censure this leader for not being "forceful enough." Dan also undervalues his interpersonal abilities and sticks to the tasks of business when describing his strengths.

Jim Stevens worries about not being "dynamic" enough. He attempts to practice a management style that is open and allows subordinates a measure of leeway, yet he is inconsistent in this practice. Like Dan Monroe, he plays down his affiliative qualities that co-workers admire.

The educational leaders, Paul Meyer and Herb Weiss, have adopted the anti-macho ideologies of their organizations and make a point of *not* being like the male stereotype. Paul censures himself for those moments when the workload becomes so demanding that he must be production rather than people-oriented in order to get the task done. Yet co-workers admire his capacity for organizing and producing a large volume of work.

Herb focuses on his interpersonal skills and sensitivities. He is largely unaware of the authority and power that he holds in the eyes of his co-workers. While he is criticized by both himself and his co-workers for being too lenient, he also worries about becoming too authoritarian.

The social service directors also evidence an effort to disassociate themselves from the macho image with variable results. Joe Ryan views himself as less dominant and more affiliative than do his co-workers. He prides himself on his openness and sensitivity. Even his weakness, becoming too personally involved in work issues, is discrepant with the male managerial tradition. Yet he sometimes has lapses of losing his openness.

Ron Smith also distinguishes himself from this tradition with some success. He criticizes himself for a lack of toughness in firing and handling conflict situations, yet he is concerned about maintaining good relations with his staff. Compared to co-workers he views himself as being more directive in some ways and less directive in other ways.

The issue of the prevalence of sex stereotypes will be discussed further following the discussion of the self-perceptions of the women leaders in Chapter Six.

NOTES

1.   The Interpersonal Check List (LaForge and Suczek, 1955).

2.   The Leader Behavior Description Questionnaire—Form XII (Ohio State leadership Studies, 1962).

3.   The theory that "self-confrontation," the presentation of information concerning one's own and significant others' attitudes and behaviors, leads to behavior and attitudinal changes is widely supported by research (e.g., Greenstein, 1976; Rokeach and McLellan, 1972). The theory is generally attributed to Rokeach as presented in *The Nature of Human Values* (1973).

The technique of feedback and confrontation meetings is widely used by organization development practitioners as a method for facilitating change in organizations (Huse, 1979).

4.   Throughout this chapter several closely related terms are used interchangeably.   These terms include: self-knowledge, self-acceptance, self-awareness, self-perception, self-disclosure, self-reflection, self-contemplation.   All of these terms refer to the state of knowing oneself as others do.

CHAPTER SIX: WOMEN VIEW THEMSELVES AS LEADERS

> "If practice at spontaneous self-disclosure promotes insight and empathy, then perhaps we have here one of the mechanisms by which women become more adept at these aspects of their so-called "expressive" role. Women, trained toward motherhood and a comforting function, both engage in and receive more self-disclosure than men."
>
> Sidney Jourard, *The Transparent Self*

Letters reporting the results of the leadership study to the six female leaders are presented next. The business women are presented first: Eileen Grant, sales manager at the travel agency and Carol Victor, project director in a large, private corporation. Next are the educational leaders: Mary Duncan, administrator for the school district, and Rose Lerner, university department head. Finally the social service leaders are presented: Susan Baker, alcoholism clinic director and Anne Ferrari, director of the criminal justice agency. Following the reports of these women is a discussion which draws on comparisons of the ways that men and women view themselves as leaders.

Dear Eileen Grant: (Sales Manager, Travel Agency)

You requested a report on the leadership study that was conducted at the travel agency. Specifically, you asked for feedback on differences between the way you describe your management and the way co-workers (subordinates, peers and superiors) described you. I am writing to respond to this request, but have little to say on the subject. Your perceptions are remarkably accurate and discrepancies are small. What information there is, however, may be enlightening to you.

Let me begin by reviewing the two interpersonal style profiles, one which represents your self perceptions and another which represents a composite view of your leadership in the eyes of co-workers. On three of the dimensions of this profile, the scores are nearly identical: on the dominant, hostile and affiliative dimensions. Only on the submissive dimension is there a discrepancy. Compared to the profile that co-workers drew, you see yourself as being more submissive.

This result reminds me of a comment that you made in your interview. I had asked you to list your weaknesses as a leader and you began by saying, "If something is not done right away, I will step in and do it." I was struck by your considering this a weakness because one of your co-workers had given a nearly identical description of your *strengths*: "If there is a problem she will step in and pick up the ball." In your more submissive view of yourself, such interventions may seem overly directive. To your co-workers, however, this assertive behavior seems appropriate indeed!

Other comments from your interview indicate that your "submissiveness" may be positively valued. Some of the strengths which you mention are your being "a little soft," able to "get along with [your] staff" and capable of "delegating responsibility." But you also value your dynamic side and see yourself as enjoying aspects of your work such as "trouble shooting," "directing," "taking on challenges." Furthermore you see yourself as "intelligent" in the performance of these activities.

Co-workers also cite "soft" and dynamic qualities in enumerating your strengths as a leader. On the soft side they agree that you are able to "get along with other people," "talk to anyone" and be "pleasant." On the dynamic side they agree that you are "quick," "make decisions decisively," have the "strength of your convictions" and "give more than 100% as a leader and as an employee."

The weakness which is most frequently cited by co-workers concerns your personal situation—the divorce which you were going through at the time the information was gathered from the travel agency. Co-workers mentioned that you took long lunch breaks and were critical that your personal life was interfering with your work. They feared that you may not be "dependable," and thought that you were setting a "bad example" for your staff.

This subtle erosion of your authority in the eyes of co-workers is evident in the scoring of the Role Assumption Scale. On three items the discrepancy between your self-rating and co-workers' ratings is considerable.[1] On all three of these most discrepant items, your self-rating is higher. Compared to co-workers, you see yourself as failing to take necessary action less often, letting your travel agents have authority you should keep less often, and as being easily recognized as the leader of the group more often.

Similarly on the Initiating Structure Scale two of the most discrepant items are scored higher when you are rating yourself: #7) "She makes sure that her part in the group is understood by group members," and #10) "She asks that group members follow standard rules and regulations."

The most discrepant item on the Initiating Structure Scale, however, is scored much lower by yourself, and relates to the more submissive way that you described yourself on the style profile: #5) "She decides what shall be done and how it shall be done." While you think that you "seldom" make such decisions, co-workers think that you do it "often."

In sum, co-workers appreciated you both for your ability to be directive and for the fact that you can be "a little soft." Perceptions differ in two ways. First, co-workers view you as being slightly more directive than you view yourself, especially in the area of deciding what shall be done and how it shall be done. Second, co-workers view you as having somewhat less legitimacy as a leader at this point in time because of problems in your personal life. They believe that these problems are impinging on your work.

If this report is not perfectly clear, please let me know. I would be happy to discuss it with you at length.

Sincerely yours,

Trudy Heller

Dear Carol Victor: (Project Director in a large, private corporation)

   As agreed in our contract, I am writing to provide you with feedback on the information gathered during the leadership study. Specifically, I am going to report to you on how your personal view of your job as Project Director compares to the view of your co-workers. I know that you are familiar with the questionnaire used in the study, so I shall begin without further introduction.

   I shall first discuss the interpersonal style profiles, one that represents your self-perceptions and the other representing co-workers' viewpoint. Both you and your co-workers conceive of your interpersonal style as primarily affiliative and dominant. The combination can be called a nurturing style. One of your comments describes the posture of the parent who encourages independence, "I force them to do things on their own if I think they can. Even if I could do it better it's better for them to give it a shot." At the same time you provide limits and guidance: "I make a habit of telling people exactly what's required of them, giving them feedback. I tell them how it [their work] relates to the rest of the company." This ability to provide both freedom and limits is valued positively as a strength by both yourself and your co-workers.

   This general agreement concerning the basic strength of your leadership is reiterated in the scoring of the Role Assumption Scale. Here you and your co-workers generally agree on a relatively high score— although you rate yourself slightly higher. Only one item has any remarkable discrepancy: #4) "She lets some members take advantage of her." Co-workers think that you are taken advantage of slightly more often than you do.

   A greater discrepancy is seen on the Initiating Structure Scale. In accord with your statement that you tell people "exactly what is required of them," you rate yourself close to the highest possible score on this scale.[2] Co-workers, however, think that you do considerably less of four things. These activities are: encouraging the use of uniform procedures, deciding what shall be done and how it shall be done, maintaining definite standards of performance and asking that your subordinates follow standards rules and regulations. In other words, you see yourself as being more controlling but no less legitimate a leader than do your co-workers.

On the subject of your weaknesses as a leader, both you and your co-workers talk about "frustration." The difference is that you attribute the frustration to your staff members, and they attribute the frustration to you. In other words the problem is: "I'm a lot slower to point out poor performance than I could be. Sometimes my people get frustrated because I don't step in soon enough." On the other hand, co-workers describe the situation as follows: "She's so good that when she finds something she can't do she gets a little frustrated." "She might try to teach something over her head before investigating the situation."

While everyone agrees that your weakness lies in a tendency to "not step in soon enough," explanations differ. You state that you are holding back because of a belief in allowing staffers to work things out on their own, as an educational experience. Co-workers, however, attribute your hesitation to intervene as a lack of knowledge or expertise.

This difference of interpretation reminds me of one of the general conclusions of the study which applies to women working in business organizations. I suspect that you know this already: Women are seen as incompetent until proven capable.

Respectfully yours,

Trudy Heller

Dear Mary Duncan: (Administrator for the School District)

I am writing to report to you on the results of the leadership study. When asked to describe your strengths as a school administrator, one of your first comments was that you encourage your subordinates to be honest with you. I know, therefore, that you expect this report to be honest as well. I also know that you do what you say you do because there is little difference between the way you see yourself and the way others see you performing your leadership role. You evidently are successful in listening to feedback.

Other comments from your interview elaborate on the theme of good interpersonal relations both inside and outside your office. You state that you "try to be open" and have instituted "a formal staff meeting once a week" as a vehicle for keeping channels of communication open. You also mention your connections throughout the school system: "I have good interpersonal relations with many people in the school district. I keep in touch with many areas in the city."

Another theme that emerges in your description of your strengths as a leader is a conception of yourself as egalitarian. You state that you "try to be fair." You also state that, while you expect your subordinates to work hard, you "wouldn't expect them to do more than I would. I'm a hard worker myself."

Your co-workers share the view of you as committed to fostering an open atmosphere within your office, as being well connected in the school system and as being democratic and fair. In addition, they see you as having the strengths of organization and knowledge.

On the question of your weakness as a leader there is, likewise, much commonality in your own descriptions and comments of your co-workers. Comments of co-workers concur with your criticism of yourself as being too responsible: "They [staffers] feel I take on too much . . . . If someone cries for help I jump. I should look at schedules so people don't pull in ten different directions." Co-workers also concur with your comment that you "take a mothering role with them [subordinates]." They even agree with the negative consequence of this style: "It's very hard on me when I have to critique them." In their words, "if she were a little more forceful she could say, 'That's a lousy idea.'"

The extent of this weakness appears greater to co-workers than to yourself. These differences are brought out in the most discrepant items on the Role Assumption amd Initiating Structure Scales. Co-workers indicate that you are more "hesitant about taking initiative in the group" than you do. They think that you try out ideas in the group less often than you do. Furthermore they think that you back down when you ought to stand firm more often than you do.

On the other hand, the problem of taking too much work appears greater to you than to co-workers. This can be seen in the discrepancies in the style profiles drawn by yourself and your co-workers. While both profiles emphasize the affiliative nature of your interpersonal style, co-workers see this dimension as being nearly equally part responsibleness and part working cooperatively. In your view, however, very little work is done cooperatively and you indicate that you bear an extreme amount of responsibility—like a mother?

To summarize briefly, relative to other leaders in the study, including your male counterpart, there is little discrepancy between your self-perceptions and perceptions of co-workers concerning your leadership. Two points which do indicate remarkable dicrepancies are as follows: 1) You see youself as personally bearing more responsibility than do co-workers; 2) co-workers see you as being less assertive and forceful than you see youself.

Please feel free to call if all of this information is not clear.

Cordially,

Trudy Heller

Dear Rose Lerner: (University Department Head)

Here is the report on the leadership study that was conducted in your department at the University. We have spoken at great length on the topic, participatory management. Learning of your enthusiasm for this style, I am not surprised to see these inclinations reflected in your self-perceptions as measured by the instruments of the leadership study.

Let me begin by reminding you of the strengths you reported in your interview. All concern your participatory style. In your words: "I am a participatory leader (groups make better decisions than only one person)." You proceed to define your terms: "I transmit what expected outcomes are and they [subordinates] figure out how to do it." Finally you describe the positive outcomes of this method: "It works. It elicits commitment. They [your faculty members] go beyond."

Your co-workers concur completely with this description of your strengths. They agree that groups make better decisions: "She draws on the staff and others possessing expertise." They agree that you transmit your expectations: "She provides structure for the work that has to done." They agree that the method elicits commitment: "Her leadership is contagious. You get involved with her interests."

The discrepancies which show up between your self-perceptions and those of co-workers concern the weaknesses of the participatory method. You are aware that "It's time consuming," i.e., group decision-making, and that "It's difficult for a newcomer to understand the process." The discrepancy is, first, in the extent to which you practice a facilitative style of management. This can be seen on the nine items (out of 20) on the Role Assumption and Initiating Structure Scales which showed considerable discrepancies between your self-scores and co-workers' scores. All discrepant items are similar in indicating that you see yourself as being considerably less directive than do your co-workers.

The most discrepant items on the Role Assumption Scale indicate that co-workers see you retaining more authority than you do. You indicate that you often let other persons take away your leadership in the group. Co-workers, on the other hand, indicate that you almost never do this. Similarly, you indicate that you often let some members take away authority you should keep. Co-workers, however, indicate that you seldom or never are so non-directive. The same pattern of discrepancies exists to a lesser extent on items #8) "She takes full charge when emergencies arise," #9) "She overcomes attempts to challenge her leadership," item #10) "She is easily recognized as the leader of the group," and item #4) "She lets some members take advantage of her." On each of these items, co-workers see you as being more authoritarian than you see yourself.

On the Initiating Structure Scale, the same pattern prevails. Others think that you often "assign group members to particular tasks," whereas you think that you seldom do this. You indicate that you never "decide what shall be done and how it should be done" whereas others think that you occasionally or often make such assignments. In terms of scheduling the work to be done, again, the same pattern occurs. You say that you occasionally do the scheduling. Others think that you do this often or always.

This pattern is also confirmed by differences in the interpersonal style profiles drawn by yourself and by your co-workers. Co-workers see you as being primarily affiliative and secondarily submissive. You see yourself, however, as being primarily submissive and secondarily affiliative (the reverse). The greatest difference is a substantial increase in the "docile" score on your profile. This change reflects the way you see yourself delagating authority to a greater extent than do co-workers.

Evidently co-workers are discerning cues from you as to how and what and when work should be done, cues which you do not intend. You think you have set them on their own, yet they are still looking to you for direction—and often finding cues to follow.

When the expected structure is not provided, however, co-workers express disapproval or disdain for the participative leadership style that you espouse. This criticism ranges from mild wishes for "tighter planning for meetings" to harsh rejection of the participatory method: "She likes group approval rather than being a leader." To summarize, I think that you are quite right when you say that your participative style is "difficult for a newcomer to understand." I hope that this report may serve to explain the extent and nature of that misunderstanding, and thereby be helpful to you.

Cordially,

Trudy Heller

Dear Susan Baker: (Alcoholism Clinic Director)

The report that I promised you is finally finished and I am hastening to get it in the mail to you. I would be very interested in receiving your reactions to it, so please feel free to write or call if you have any questions or comments for me.

Let me begin by reminding you of the strengths and weaknesses you attributed to yourself as clinic director in your interview. You stated first that you are "perceptive" and then you elaborated upon this idea. You mentioned that you have a "clear idea of [your own] needs" and that you are "good at knowing others' strengths and weaknesses." You described yourself as not only perceptive about people but also organizational dynamics. As an organizational problem solver you can "analyse clearly and quickly" and "see alternatives to problems." Another aspect of your perceptiveness is that you are aware when a decision has gone awry. In your own words, you can "recoup when there is a mess . . . using resources, people, and money."

Two additional strengths complete your list. You cite your skill in building an "atmosphere of trust" and in "fostering creativity." On the final item, you were uncertain whether to classify this characteristic as a strength or a weakness (you will see that your co-workers have an opinion about this question of classification), the characteristic of not over-identifying with the organization."

The weaknesses that you ascribe to your leadership are generally on the theme of being either too aggressive or too non-assertive. When you are too aggressive you "like to get people to do things that *I* want" and/or you are "overprotective of others." On the other hand, you describe a weakness of non-assertion. "Sometimes its hard to ask people to do things."

Do co-workers (subordinates, peers and superiors) corroborate these conceptions of the strengths and weak-nesses of your leadership? Generally speaking there is little difference between your view of yourself and co-workers' view of you as clinic director. On both leadership style profiles (yours and the others) your style is seen as being predominantly affiliative and dominant —with a nearly equal emphasis on these two interpersonal modes.

Similarly, on the Role Assumption and Initiating Struc-ture Scales discrepancies are small. On the Role Assumption Scale you generally rate yourself lower than do your co-workers. On the two most discrepant items this is the case: #4) "She is never the leader of the group in name only." #10) "She is easily recognized as the leader of the group." You indicate that these items are often true, whereas co-workers felt they are always true.

On the Initiating Structure Scale, co-workers indicate their disagreement with your sense that you sometimes lack assertion. The three most discrepant items all have co-workers indicating that you provide more structure than you think you do. These three areas are: letting group members know what's expected of them, making your attitudes clear to the group, and making sure that your part in the group is understood by group members.

Comments made by your co-workers will help to explain these discrepancies. On the positive side co-workers would assure you that they "read you loud and clear." They see you as a "risk-taker" in terms of "bringing things up at meetings," that your "manner of presentation gets the point across quickly," and that you are someone who is "honest with self and others" and "doesn't keep her mouth closed."

On the negative side, I think that co-workers would disagree with your sense that you are too interfering in terms of getting people to do things that you want and hence imposing your will on them. Nor do they see you as being hesitant to ask people to do things. On the other hand, your sense that you are "sometimes overprotective of others" I think is shared. Co-workers describe this characteristic in a slightly different way, however. To them you have a tendency to "personalize things, to take things to heart, and be affected personally," "to get really involved in a situation and not maintain enough distance to have objectivity." The consensus of your co-workers is clearly that to "*not* over-identify with the organization" is a strength.

Again, please feel free to call or write of you have any questions concerning this report.

Cordially,

Trudy Heller

Dear Anna Ferrari: (Director of the Criminal Justice Agency)

Following up on our telephone conversation, I am sending you a report on the information gathered from your criminal justice agency. I shall present the information with a focus on differences and similarities between the way you see yourself as director and the way others (subordinates, peers, and superiors) see you. Other leaders that I have worked with have found that this is a useful way of looking at feedback.

I shall begin by reminding you of your own description of your strengths and weaknesses. Your description of your strengths focuses on what I call your political skills. These skills include good connections in the system outside your office. In your own words: "I have a lot of informal contacts, broad experience in the field." Another skill which may be useful both inside and outside the office is speaking ability, "ability to articulate issues and insights before others." Finally, you note that your work is based upon a genuine concern for the people who are served by your agency: "I have some feeling for human beings . . . that helps me to be effective and credible."

The major weakness which you attribute to yourself is the lack of a cogent leadership style. You articulate this issue very well: "I struggle to develop an image or style that is appropriate for a woman in this field (which has no role models) so I'm not as secure in my position as I might be. My willingness to experiment with leadership forms is both a strength and a weakness."

The one specific aspect of the leadership role which you cite as problematic is the task of firing people. When it's too difficult to fire someone you sometimes "ask others to do it." But you consider this behavior to be a weakness.

Co-workers generally agree with this self-report and yours is one of the lower discrepancy scores of the twelve leaders who participated in the study. They too cite your political strengths and the job you have done in developing your organization. They too report you are "articulate" and "perceptive about people." They too remark on your "conflicting, contradictory" style.

The discrepancy which does emerge from this information is best seen in differences between the two style profiles, one based on your self-ratings and the other based on co-workers' ratings of you. On the profile which you draw of yourself your interpersonal style is primarily dominant and concentrated in the managerial mode. On the profile which your co-workers have drawn of you, however, your style is both dominant and hostile, with an even emphasis on these two modes of interaction.

The higher dominance score on your self-perceived profile is partly explained by discrepant items on the Initiating Structure Scale. On three remarkably discrepant items, you see yourself as providing more structure than do your co-workers: in encouraging the use of uniform procedures, in making sure that your part in the group is understood by group members, and in asking that group members follow standard rules and regulations.

There were no notable discrepancies on the Role Assumption Scale. Yet on the two most discrepant items the same pattern is revealed: You see yourself as more forceful in taking charge when emergencies arise and in opposing subordinates who challenge your authority.

Co-workers' comments, however, do the most to explain how the managerial style which you intend and attribute to yourself becomes viewed as having a hostile component in the eyes of co-workers. I shall do some guessing here and try to put your situation into role theory terms. Suppose staffers expect you to be a non-authoritarian leader, allowing them a great deal of leeway in which to complete their work in their own way. If what comes naturally to you is a more authoritarian style (this may be what works best outside the agency in the political arena) you may vacillate, making concessions to their expectations (perceptive as you are) and then other times returning to a more authoritarian style. Co-workers may see such "backlashes" as having a hostile intent. Perhaps if you were not so sensitive to their expectations—strangely enough—you would be better able to consistently follow your natural inclinations and everyone would be more content in the long run.

How does this interpretation sound to you? Please let me know.

Cordially,

Trudy Heller

CONCLUSION

Are these women more self-aware as leaders than their colleagues who are men? Do they see themselves as others do? One way of answering these questions is in quantitative terms. To this end a so-called "discrepancy" score was computed for each leader.[3] This score represents the extent of the difference between a leader's personal view of his or her leadership and the viewpoint of co-workers (subordinates, peers, and superiors). The lower the score, the more the leaders see themselves as others do.

By this measure the women do tend to be more self-aware. With the exception of Carol Victor, the five other women had lower discrepancy scores than their male counterparts. This is true even in those pairs where the man could be considered the more successful leader in terms of co-workers' reports and/or Role Assumption scores, as in the cases of Anna Ferrari and Ron Smith of the Criminal Justice

Agencies (see Chapter Four) or Mary Duncan and Paul Meyer of the School District (see Chapter Three).

The influence of the organizational context also becomes apparent in examining discrepancies. Travel Agency Managers Dan Monroe and Eileen Grant are the two leaders who, as a pair, have the lowest discrepancy scores. The small size of their organization makes their travel agency a place where it is difficult to keep information secret. The mere proximity of co-workers and the cohesiveness of the group creates a climate where perceptions are likely to be shared.

At the other extreme, the pair with the highest discrepancy score is Herb Weiss and Rose Lerner, the University Department Heads. Again, organizational factors can explain this finding. The principles of academic freedom and professionalism, plus the varied work schedules of academic employees, creates a climate where faculty members are only loosely supervised by the department head. The relative lack of interaction fosters discrepancies and allows them to persist—and may not interfere with work getting done.

Another related question is whether this greater awareness is an asset or a liability to the women in performing their leadership roles. Here the exception, Project Director Carol Victor, provides an example which challenges the assumption of Homans (1950), Weick (1978) and others that more self-awareness is always better. Carol is the one female leader who has less accurate self-perceptions than her male counterpart, Jim Stevens.

Organizational factors again figure importantly into Carol's situation. Carol's organization, a large, private corporation, is the organization from the study that has the least experience with women as leaders. To be desensitized to the hostile attitudes in her environment could be very functional indeed. A lack of sensitivity to negative expectations and attitudes allows Carol to maintain a positive self-image, to maintain her confidence as a leader in the face of expectations of failure. In common language, Carol has not allowed her environment to "bring her down." If she persists in this way she may even be able to bring her co-workers up toward a more positive view of women as leaders.

Contrast the case of Project Director Victor with the case of Anna Ferrari, director of a criminal justice agency. Anna also works in a hostile environment, not because of a masculine management ethic, rather because of widespread discontent with her leadership style.   Compared to Carol, Anna is preoccupied with the negative feedback.   Her discrepancy score is lower than Carol's, yet she has become bogged down in office gossip by attending so closely to it.

In *Beyond Sex Roles,* Kanter (1977) makes the point that many of the norms of human relations training are the same as the characteristics of the stereotypical female.   One of these norms is: "learn to receive and be influenced by feedback" (Kanter, 1977, p. 383).   Furthermore, Kanter suggests, human relations training may be the *last* thing that women need:

> Thus while men may need help learning about relationships and emotional expression, women need help learning just the opposite: the experience of power, task orientation, intellectualizing, behaving 'impersonally' and addressing large groups, *invulnerability to feedback,* and other new experiences in interpersonal behavior for many women (emphasis is my own).

In addition to studying the extent of discrepancies between the leaders' self-perceptions and the perceptions of co-workers, examining the content of the discrepancies provided a rich source of information as well.   One question that can be addressed with this information is whether the leaders see themselves in terms of the sex stereotypes described in Chapter One.   Here again the organizational context matters.   Consistent with other evidence for a stronger presence of sex stereotyping in the business organizations (see Chapter Two), the four business leaders show some evidence of adhering to the standards of the stereotype for their sexes.   A pattern emerges on the most discrepant dimension of the style profile for each business leader.   For Dan Monroe, travel agency manager, the submissive is the most discrepant dimension, and Dan sees himself as less submissive (more masculine) than do his co-workers.   For Dan's fellow manager, Eileen Grant, the submissive is also the dimension where the greatest discrepancy exists.   Eileen sees herself as *more* submissive (more feminine) than do her co-workers.

In the large, private corporation, Project Directors Jim Stevens and Carol Victor both have the greatest discrepancy on the affiliative dimension. Jim sees himself as being less affiliative (more masculine) than do co-workers. Carol sees herself as more affiliative (more feminine) than her co-workers do.

In the educational and social service organizations, however, this pattern does not hold. Paul Meyer, administrator for the school district, for example, sees himself as being more affiliative than do co-workers. In the criminal justice agency, Director Anna Ferrari sees herself as more dominant than do co-workers. Consistent with the evidence presented in Chapters Three and Four, sex stereotyping is less prevalent in these organizations.

Finally, perhaps the most interesting question which is addressed by this material concerns values. Three of the leaders in the study give descriptions of an aspect of their leadership which is nearly identical to comments made by co-workers. A discrepancy exists, however, in the value placed upon the behavior in question. For example, Eileen Grant, travel agency manager, listed as a *weakness* her tendency to step in too quickly when a subordinate is having difficulty with a particular task. One of Eileen's subordinates listed as a *strength* the fact that she will "jump in and carry the ball."

Similarly, Susan Baker described herself as keeping a certain emotional and psychological distance from her job as alcoholism clinic director. She equivocated and was unable to classify this behavior as either a strength or a weakness. Several of Susan's co-workers mentioned this same behavior. They were unanimous and very clear about its classification as a strength.

Paul Meyer, administrator for the school district, notes that his weakness as a leader is that at times he is too "product oriented." He says that he slips into this kind of behavior when the pressures of the work load are great. He also criticizes himself for accepting too much work for his operation. Yet Paul's co-workers classify as strengths these same production-oriented qualities, praising him for being "hard working," "well organized," "resourceful" and "prepared." No negative comments were made by co-workers on this theme.

All three of these cases of values misclassification occur on themes that are stereotypically a part of male leader behavior.   Men are emotionally detached and objective about their workplace, men are assertive, and men are committed hard workers.   In all three cases the leaders are declaring that the "macho" behaviors are a weakness, while co-workers call the same actions a strength.   *The current value of the masculine management ethic is clearly confused and changing.*

NOTES

1.   A difference of 1.0 between leader and co-worker scores was used as a standard for selecting those items to be considered "considerably" or "remarkably" discrepant.

2.   Carol Victor's self-rated Initiating Structure Scale received a score of 4.9.   The highest possible score is 5.0. Out of ten items only one was rated below the highest possible rating, 5.

3.   The discrepancy score was derived as follows: The discrepancies on each item of the Role Assumption and Initiating Structure Scales, plus the discrepancies on each of the four dimensions of the interpersonal style profile, were simply totalled for each leader.

CHAPTER VII: LEADERS AS PEERS AND SUBORDINATES

> "Neither men nor women—however capable, however gutsy—are prepared for a business world in which the sexes meet on an equal basis. How could they be? Until recently, a female executive of a major corporation was as much of a novelty as Jackie Robinson was in major league baseball parks in 1947.
>
> As business becomes more of a two-sex world, both women and men will have to tinker with the balance of their personal and professional lives. These are questions of both style . . . and substance."
>
> Susan Jacoby, *The New York Times*, Sunday, October 19, 1980

Item: Mary Cunningham, twenty-nine year old vice president for strategic planning at the Bendix Corporation, resigns in the midst of controversy and gossip about her professional/personal relationship with her boss and Bendix Chairman, forty-three year old William Agee (Bernstein, 1980).

Item: A court decision establishes a precedent for companies who provide their executives with the "perk" of membership in a private club. The court rules that federal funds may be withheld from companies that provide memberships to clubs that exclude women. The

127

rationale for the decision is that important business transpires among peers at these "social" institutions. Therefore, exclusion of women puts them at a disadvantage and is discriminatory ("All Male Clubs . . . ", 1980).

Item: A French manager has written a best-selling novel based on his experience working in a multinational company (Pilhes, 1974). In the novel, he describes his fellow managers as "conformist subordinates." The book is especially popular among French managers on the basis of "a tremendous 'aha' effect" (Laurent, 1978).

Item: A woman scientist who is the director of a research laboratory was invited to participate in the leadership study. After some discussion she confessed that while she was comfortable with my request to gather information from her subordinates and her superior, she could not allow me to question her peers. She felt that her acceptance among her peers was too uncertain to be disturbed by such questioning.

These news items underline the importance of peer and superior relations for the manager or leader. In this Chapter I am suggesting that a leader's relations with peers and superiors is a fruitful area of exploration in the attempt to understand women and men as leaders. First I shall present evidence—both theoretical and empirical—that underlines the importance of considering leaders as peers and subordinates. By way of example, three pairs of leaders from the leadership study will then be analyzed in terms of how they are influenced by their peers and superiors. Finally, patterns of influence will be discussed with a focus on differences between the women and men.

Support for exploring superior and peer relationships comes, first, from a dilemma in leadership research. An increasing amount of evidence indicates that, in many situations, there is no significant difference between male and female leaders in their relationships with subordinates (e.g., Bartol and Wortman, 1979; Day and Stogdill, 1972; Osborn and Vicars, 1976; Shingledecker and Terborg, 1980). Yet a pyramid-shaped distribution of women in most organizations still exists whereby women are concentrated at lower levels of the organization in lower-paid, lower-status jobs. The nature of this distribution calls for an explanation. Researchers and practitioners alike are reluctant to conclude that there are no more attitudinal barriers to women entering the ranks of leadership. Conclusions are rather more cautiously phrased, in terms of simply not discovering the barriers—which presumably still exist—in the leader-subordinate relationship. A logical course to follow, then, is the exploration of superior and peer relations.

Andre Laurent (1978) of the European Institute of Business Administration points out the lack of attention paid to subordinacy and followership in the study of organizational behavior.

> "Every manager a subordinate" as a company slogan probably would be less attractive to candidates than the more glamorous book title *Every Employee A Manager* (Myers, 1970). Yet both expressions reflect a single organizational reality; if every employee is a manager, it follows that every employee—and for our purposes every manager—is also a subordinate, a follower of other leaders. Most people in work organizations, parti-cularly managers, play this dual role of leading and being led, managing and being managed. But research on subordination seems less popular than studies of leader-ship, and a managerial course on "Effective Subordination" might be difficult to sell (Laurent, 1978, p. 220).

Laurent goes on to suggest that the reason for the lack of interest in followership and subordinacy is the status and prestige which is placed on leadership in our society, and the negative value placed on subordinacy and followership.

As outsiders who have long been excluded from the status and prestige associated with positions of leadership, women may be particularly loathe to explore the phenomenon of subordinacy. Women reacted strongly, for example, to the publication of Daniel Levinson's work, *Seasons of a Man's Life* (1978), and the subsequent popularization of his concept of the mentor—a special kind of superior.

According to Levinson (1978) a mentor who guides one's career through early adulthood is almost essential to success.

Many women who are excluded from "old boy" networks and have few role models to follow feel that they do not have access to mentoring relationships. They objected to the idea that mentors are essential, and have set about the task of revising this concept to include women (Fury, 1980; Shapiro, et al., 1978; Spector, 1980).

While women may be reluctant to view themselves as subordinates, substantial evidence exists for the importance of supervisor support for successful women in management. In Hennig and Jardim's (1977) study of twenty-five successful women executives a patterned relationship with superiors emerged. These women typically entered the organization at the level of secretary or administrative assistant, became attached to a particular boss and were promoted through the organizational hierarchy with him. These women attributed their success largely to the support of this superior.

Another issue which points out both the importance and problematic nature of peer and superior relations for women and men in management is the issue of sexuality. Sexuality here is defined as "the various ways in which a male manager sees himself as a sexual male and responds to the sexuality of a female co-worker and the ways a female manager experiences her own sexuality in responding to males" (Bradford, et al., 1975, p. 41). The task of separating work and social roles (one of the strengths attributed to men in Chapter One) is obviously a great deal easier if work is a man's world—with the exception of women as secretaries and other low-status personnel.

The introduction of women into management level positions complicates peer relations. Bradford, et al., describe the far-reaching consequences of this issue: " . . . sexuality in one form or another helps to explain why managers feel ambivalent about affirmative action for women, why many men and women have difficulty relating to one another in the office, and women executives are handicapped in their search for success" (p. 41).

The consequences are far-reaching and negative because traditionally the issue of sexuality in the workplace has been mismanaged. The result of this mismanagement is that either women and men have been limited by several stereotypical male-female interactions which, at best, foster dependence—not competence—in the woman. Kanter's (1976) negative stereotypes of women which were discussed in Chapter One such as "pet," "sex object" and "mother" are examples of the stereotyped roles that women may play in interactions with men.

At worst sexual issues emerge in the form of sexual harassment of women. While this is a difficult topic to research, Harragan (1977) states her belief that "more women are refused employment, fired or forced to quit salaried jobs as a result of sexual demands and the ramifications thereof than for any other single cause" (p. 366). A cover story on the topic, sexual harassment, in *Ms. Magazine* (November, 1977) makes two points that are particularly salient to women in management. One is that harassment is not limited to women in lower-level positions: "Clearly the power of one's job is not a protection from sexual harassment. It may make men want to 'conquer' even more" (Lindsey, 1977, p. 75).

The other point is that harassment may come from peers as well as a superior: "Although most sexual harassment of women on the job comes from bosses and supervisors—those with direct economic power over the women—this is not the only pattern of harassment. A lot also comes from male co-workers, whose behavior is tacitly or openly sanctioned by their supervisor . . .." (Lindsey, 1977, p. 75).

In sum, peer and superior relations are important to women and men as leaders for the following reasons. One set of reasons, coming from the mainstream of organizational behavior research, is the lack of attention paid to the topic. Another set of reasons, coming from the recent literature on women in management, is the issue of sexuality in peer and superior relations in a coeducational workplace.

Three pairs of leaders will next be discussed with a focus on differences in the ways the leaders are viewed by subordinates, peers and superiors. The three pairs were selected because a complete set of data, including interviews with peers and superiors, was available for each leader. While the information provided by the leadership study does not permit discussion of mentor relationships or the issue of sexuality, basic patterns of identification and influence can be discerned in the cases of Jim Stevens and Carol Victor, corporate project directors, school district administators, Paul Meyer and Mary Duncan, and small business managers Dan Monroe and Eileen Grant.

PROJECT DIRECTORS: JIM STEVENS AND CAROL VICTOR

Jim Stevens and Carol Victor are project directors in a large, private corporation. Since their company is designed as a matrix organization, Jim and Carol are each assigned a staff to supervise for the duration of a particular project. At the conclusion of a project staff members and directors may be reassigned to a new project. Jim and Carol share the same boss who is head of their department.

In several ways Jim and Carol are different. While Jim has been with the company for seventeen years, Carol has been employed for just one year. Jim is thirty-seven years old; Carol is twenty-four. All of Jim's co-workers who participated in the study (including subordinates, peers and superiors) are white males and married. Carol also works among predominantly male co-workers, but she has one female subordinate and one female peer. Her co-workers represent a variety of marital statuses. Average numbers of years of seniority is one and one-half for Carol's subordinates and peers and is ten for Jim's subordinates and peers. In sum, although Carol and Jim differ in terms of age, seniority and sex, their work groups differ along these same dimensions.

Jim Stevens

Beginning with the interpersonal style profile and comparing the three perspectives of Jim's subordinates, peers and superiors reveals some interesting contrasts. To subordinates Jim is primarily affiliative and secondarily dominant.

When asked to describe Jim's strengths as a leader, subordinates emphasize his interpersonal abilities (his affiliativeness) and his expertise (the basis of his dominance). Interpersonally, he is described by subordinates as "very concerned," "very honest, sincere" "easy to work with." As a supervisor he is "helpful" and "always open to new ideas." In his openness, "he doesn't always follow the organized method —if it sounds good, he'll try it." Jim is also appreciated for leading "by example." Subordinates say that "he is not afraid to get his hands dirty."

Jim's expertise reportedly comes from having had "a lot of experience." "He knows what should be done and how to approach it." Furthermore, "if he doesn't know the answer, he'll find someone who does. He has contacts in every department, key men he can go to."

Subordinates decline to describe any weaknesses in their leader, yet of the three groups, subordinates, peers, superiors, they give him the lowest rating on the Role Assumption and Initiating Structure Scales. While it is understandable that subordinates who are most vulnerable to a leader's power would be the most reluctant to reveal any weaknesses of this leader, they do not seem to be covering up a great deal of negative information. Rather, they seem to see Jim as a pretty nice guy to work for.

Compared to subordinates, however, Jim's peers appear to be his greatest supporters. The profile which peers draw of Jim is the most like the tough male stereotype. He is more dominant than submissive and more hostile than affiliative. He is considerably less submissive in the eyes of his peers than in the view of subordinates. This submissive dimension has the greatest discrepancy.

Jim's peers also give him the highest scores on the Role Assumption and Initiating Structure Scales. Peers emphasize Jim's expertise and capacity to produce quality work in describing his strengths: "He is very knowledgeable in his field." "He understands many facets of the business." "He has tremendous ability to get into a project that he knows very little about and get to know the details very well—and quickly, too."

The criticism that peers have of Jim's leadership is of a tendency to be "overcautious:" "He overchecks before offering an opinion." He has "a tendency toward indecision caused by a fear of offending someone." Furthermore, Jim is "a little bit too touchy when you disagree with him. He's very upset when you talk to someone else about it."

Jim's superior, however, is the most critical when compared to subordinates and peers. The interpersonal style profile that he draws of Jim is primarily (and extremely) hostile and secondarily dominant. The profile has Jim depicted as having almost no submissiveness and very little affiliation.

Consistent with the high dominance score of the profile are Jim's boss's remarks. He cites Jim's assertiveness as his primary strength. He describes Jim as "intelligent," as having "a great deal of initiative," as someone who can "carry things through without being told what to do." Furthermore, on most occasions, he "shows good judgement."

The boss's criticisms of Jim are consistent with the high hostility score on the profile. "He can become terribly hard on the people who work with him as far as not giving them too much leeway—tends toward pigheadedness." Jim's boss attributes this tendency to an over-involvement in his work: "He tends to become personally involved in his project to the point where he's emotionally, ego-involved in his work."

In sum, Jim is viewed most favorably by his peers. This group draws a style profile of Jim which is most like the tough and dominant male stereotype. Peers also give Jim his highest score on the Role Assumption Scale. Subordinates are a close second to peers in being supportive of Jim's leadership. Subordinates, however, focus more on Jim's affiliativeness, his "people skills." Compared to the other two groups, Jim's boss is the most critical. He sees a strong hostile tendency in his leader.

Carol Victor

Comparing the different perspectives of Carol Victor's subordinates, peers and superiors indicates that her greatest supporters are her subordinates. The style profile that they draw of her emphasizes the dominant and submissive dimensions. The subordinates, furthermore, are the group which gives Carol the highest ratings on both the Role Assumption and Initiating Structure Scales. They also are the group which has the highest score on the measure of attitudes toward women (Peters, Terborg and Taynor, 1974) indicating that the attitudes of subordinates are the most positive toward women assuming managerial roles.

Comments of subordinates concerning Carol's strengths as a leader focus on her interpersonal abilities and her intelligence. Specifically, subordinates describe her ability to be a leader in spite of attitudinal barriers for her as a woman: "She comes across very easily and has no problems, no social barriers that other people may have." In another subordinate's words: "She doesn't seem to differentiate or be inhibited by sex-role stereotypes. She manages very well to deal with situations that come up."

The other characteristic attributed to Carol by subordinates, her intelligence, is the key to the weakness that this group sees in their leader. They think that she sometimes gets into work that is over her head. Having difficulty acknowledging her limits, she sometimes "gets a little frustrated."

Carol's peers share the view expressed by subordinates that she is "bright." They elaborate on this quality, describing her as "conscientious," "hardworking," "organized" and as "taking an activist role rather than a passive one."

Peers, however, have a different view of Carol's weakness as a leader. She sometimes fails to communicate with her peer group. In their words, "Her weakness might be in communication skills being fairly vague. She sometimes can't keep other people informed of her output, of her results."

This communications gap may, however, be related to a characteristic of Carol's peer group. Peers received a lower rating on the measure of attitudes toward women (Peters, Terborg, and Taynor, 1974) than Carol's subordinates who praise her for her ability to relate. The peer group's more negative attitudes toward women may create some interference in the communications process with Carol.

Peers differentiate, however, between Carol's communication style with them and her style with her subordinates. On the interpersonal style profile peers describe Carol as primarily affiliative. Although they criticize her for failing to communicate adequately with them, peers believe that with subordinates Carol is primarily affiliative.

One final criticism from peers comes from the leader behavior scales, Role Assumption and Initiating Structure. The peer group gives Carol her lowest scores on both of these scales. They view her as having the least legitimacy as a leader and as providing the lowest amount of structure for her subordinates.

Still another view of Carol's leadership comes from her boss. He focuses on Carol's ability to relate to and motivate her staff in describing her strengths: "Her primary strength is her ability to get people to work with her by being neither overbearing nor meek, but by being cheerful and enthusiastic and willing to work hard." The only weakness her boss describes is her "inexperience because she's young."

The style profile that Carol's superior draws of her is primarily dominant and secondarily affiliative. He rates her lower on the Role Assumption Scale compared to subordinates, and higher compared to peers. His rating on the Initiating Structure Scale is the same as subordinates and higher than the peers. His score on the measure of attitudes toward women assuming leadership roles, however, is as low as the score received by Carol's peers.

In sum, Carol's boss appears to be generally supportive of her. His description carefully distinguishes her from the negative stereotypes of female leaders, being neither "too meek" nor "too overbearing." He admires her for forging a new style and sees her as lacking only in experience.

Carol's greatest supporters, however, appear to be her subordinates. They give her the highest ratings on the Role Assumption and Initiating Structure Scales. They have the most positive attitudes toward women. Their comments include praise for Carol's interpersonal as well as her task-oriented skills.

Her weakest supporters appear to be the peer group. They give her the lowest score on the Role Assumption and Initiating Structure Scales. They describe her as having communication difficulties and their profile of her is the most stereotypically feminine, i.e., she is viewed as primarily affiliative.

SCHOOL DISTRICT ADMINISTRATORS PAUL MEYER AND MARY DUNCAN

Paul Meyer and Mary Duncan are administrators for the school district. Their situations are similar in several ways. Both administrators are fairly senior and they are close in age. Paul, however, is in the situation of being a member of the white male majority among his peers. Mary, on the other hand, has an all-female staff of subordinates (racially mixed) but an all-white male group of peers as well as a white male boss. The composition of these groups affects the different perceptions of these leaders.

Paul Meyer

Subordinates draw a profile of Paul Meyer which is primarily affiliative. They also depict him as equally dominant and submissive, and give him a low hostility score. Comments of subordinates tend to elaborate this profile. They emphasize first his personality and his ability to supervise without being too domineering. They state that he treats them as individuals and understands his subordinates' particular needs: "He uses good psychology. For example, if a person is interested in experimenting, he'll allow it. If he sees that the person is not interested, he'll set limits."

For all of his sensitivity and concern for people, however, Paul is "not a buddy." He keeps his distance from subordinates. "He wants to motivate you to do the best you can. He respects the decisions you make; suggests, but won't impose."

In sum, subordinates see Paul as being first of all a supervisor who is easy to relate to, who understands their needs and motivates them to work. In their view, he has a balance of dominance and submissiveness: "He can suggest but won't impose." The subordinates, furthermore, testify to their support for this administrator by giving him his highest rating on the Role Assumption Scale.

Peers have a slightly different view of Paul. They depict him on the style profile as equally dominant and affiliative, somewhat less submissive compared to subordinates and equally low on hostility compared to subordinates. In comments peers emphasize the balance Paul's leadership has in terms of task- and people-orientation. "He's very human in his approaches and given to successful completion of tasks." In meetings with peers Paul is known for being "knowledgeable," as being always "totally prepared," and as being an "excellent speaker." For all of his expertise he "never dominates" but rather "works as a part of a group." Like the subordinates, peers also decline to cite any weakness in the administration of Paul Meyer.

Paul's superior is the most critical of this leader. He gives Paul his lowest Role Assumption score. He even mentions one weakness in Paul's administration. He states that Paul sometimes does "not make decisions quickly enough." This criticism is reflected in the interpersonal style profile as primarily submissive.

He concurs with peers' view of Paul as equally affiliative and dominant and describes in his comments a similar balance of task- and people-oriented skills: "He's intelligent, analytical . . . he's dedicated;" he also "relates well to people, has sympathy, warmth."

In sum, comparing the three perspectives of subordinates, peers and superiors indicates that subordinates maintain the most favorable view of Paul's leadership. The peer group is also supportive of Paul's leadership—although somewhat less than subordinates. Finally, the most critical view comes from Paul's boss.

Mary Duncan

For Mary Duncan, subordinates, peers and superiors are distinctly different groups.   Mary's subordinates are all women (two are black and one is white). Her peers as well as her boss, however, are all white males.

Compared to the other groups, Mary's subordinates support her only moderately. This group of women gives Mary a score on the Role Assumption Scale which is greater than peers' but lower than Mary's boss's rating. Similarly, on the measure of attitudes toward women, subordinates' score indicates that their attitudes are more positive than the attitudes of Mary's peer group, but less positive than the attitudes of Mary's male boss.

The style profile that subordinates draw of Mary is consistent with the "motherly" attribution which she gives to herself. Her all-female subordinates see her as primarily— and extremely—affiliative and secondarily dominant. (The affiliative score is twice that of the dominant score.)

Comments of subordinates focus on Mary's strengths of dedication to her work, her ability to get along with people both inside and outside the office and the fact that she "gives workers some space" in which to do their work as they see fit.   Subordinates give Mary her lowest rating on the Initiating Structure Scale.

The weakness cited by subordinates is Mary's tendency to "try to please everyone." One specific consequence of this effort is that Mary has difficulty saying "no" to requests for work from her office. In the words of subordinates, she "tries to tackle too many things."

Like Carol Victor, Mary's peers could be described as her greatest critics. Of the three groups, subordinates, peers and superiors, this group of men has the lowest score on the measure of attitudes toward women, indicating they have the least positive attitudes.   They also give Mary her lowest score on the Role Assumption Subscale.

The interpersonal style profile that peers draw of Mary fits the stereotype of the female leader who is too soft and non-assertive to be an effective leader. Peers draw a profile of Mary which is primarily and largely affiliative and secondarily submissive.

Their comments expand upon these scores. They describe her weaknesses: "She's such a kind individual that some people may take advantage of her." She's also described as not being "forceful" enough in presenting her ideas and pursuing her goals: "She'll change her whole goal if someone is stronger, more forceful than her . . . if she were a little more forceful she could say 'That's a lousy idea.'" Hence, in spite of the fact that Mary is "knowledgeable," "organized," and "responsible" in the eyes of peers, her authority and power as a leader is the least well legitimized by this group.

In contrast to the peer group and even to the subordinate group, Mary's superior appears to be her greatest supporter. He gives her her highest score on the Role Assumption Subscale, and the boss himself receives the highest rating of the three status groups on the measures of attitudes toward women, indicating he has the most positive attitudes toward women assuming leadership roles.

The interpersonal style profile that Mary's boss draws of her is, furthermore, the most favorable. While the affiliative dimension gets the highest score, as with peers and superiors, this score is less extreme. The affiliative dimension is almost equal to the second highest, the dominant dimension. The boss gives Mary extremely low submission and hostility scores.

The boss's comments flesh out these measures. The boss describes this woman whom he considers to be a strong leader: "I think that as a leader she is fantastic at taking charge of projects and giving them leadership and follow-through . . . " The boss sees the same weakness that is described by subordinates and peers: "She tends to bend over backwards to accommodate people and at times she doesn't delegate enough." Yet from the boss's point of view, these weaknesses are not as serious, do not undermine Mary's power and authority as a leader to the extent that they do for subordinates and, especially, for peers.

SMALL BUSINESS MANAGERS: DAN MONROE AND EILEEN GRANT

Dan Monroe and Eileen Grant, travel agency managers, present a somewhat different picture of peer and superior views of leaders. In their small organization, they are each other's only peers. The owner of the travel agency that employs them is their common boss. The patterns of influence are therefore different under these circumstances.

Dan Monroe

Subordinates clearly have the most favorable view of Dan's managerial leadership. On subordinates' interpersonal style profile Dan is viewed as primarily dominant and affiliative, and slightly more affiliative than dominant. This group also gives Dan his highest score on the Role Assumption and Initiating Structure Scales.

Dan's peer, Manager Grant, and his boss, however, draw profiles of Dan that, while remarkably similar to each other, are considerably different from the profile of subordinates. On the profiles of his peer and boss, Dan is extremely submissive and also very affiliative. The dominant score on the peer's profile is low, and on the boss's profile the dominant score is extremely low. Dan's peer and fellow manager gives him his lowest Role Assumption score and the Role Assumption score ascribed by his boss is also far below the rating of subordinates. Hence two strikingly different perceptions of Manager Monroe emerge: One is the more favorable perception of Dan's subordinates. The other is the shared, more critical perception of Dan's peer and superior.

In view of striking differences in these two perceptions of Dan, comments made by people of all three status groups are remarkably similar. In this small organization, subordinates are aware that Dan is "a weak leader" when it comes to "approaching the owner about things he would like to see." Still to them he is a "nice guy," "easy to work for," "not demanding" and "not strict."

To Dan's boss, however, this leniency and lack of performance pressure is a more negative quality. It is a sign that Dan is "insecure," "lacks initiative," that he is even "afraid of his employees." Furthermore, Dan's peer, Manager Grant, concurs with her boss in this appraisal.

Eileen Grant

For Dan Monroe's colleague and fellow manager, a different pattern of influence emerges. Unlike Dan, whose greatest support group is his subordinates, Eileen's most favorable portrait is drawn by her superior. The boss's style profile is most similar to the one that Eileen draws of herself. It is primarily dominant and secondarily affiliative. The boss also gives Eileen her highest score on the Role Assumption Scale.

The comments of her supervisor are filled with praise for this "strong leader." In the boss's eye, Eileen "controls the people she employs." Furthermore, she "wants to advance" and is able to "take risks" and "take heat" in her ambition. He finds nothing to criticize.

In both her peer's and her subordinates' profiles, however, a hostile element is more prominent. To subordinates Eileen is primarily affiliative but secondarily hostile. This group gives her her lowest Role Assumption score. Subordinates are also the group with the least positive attitudes toward women in management.

Consistent with Eileen's affiliative rating, the subordinate group describes Eileen's interpersonal strengths. She is "able to get along with people," "can talk to anyone." She has a "pleasant" personality and "doesn't get ruffled." Consistent with the hostility score, however, Eileen can be stubborn. In the words of a subordinate, "She gets set on an idea and won't give in."

Eileen's peer, Manager Monroe, describes her as primarily hostile and secondarily dominant and affiliative— not too unlike the "iron maiden" stereotype. He blandly describes her strength as a leader: "She knows what has to be done and lets her people know what has to be done."

The weakness which is unanimously reported by peer and subordinates alike is Eileen's practice of leaving the office for hours at a time without informing her co-workers of her destination and time of return. This behavior sustained rumors about her personal life and pending divorce. The unannounced absence also evoked criticism of Eileen for "lack of dependability" and for "setting a bad example." Eileen's boss is alone in not raising this criticism.

To summarize the situation for Managers Monroe and Grant in this small organization, Dan Monroe is most favorably viewed by his subordinates. His peer and his boss share a more criticial view of his management. Consistent with this finding that Eileen and her boss join together in this view of Dan, Eileen's boss is her strongest supporter. Compared to her boss, Eileen's peer and subordinates view her more critically.

CONCLUSION

Patterns of influence emerge from these cases. Each leader is perceived somewhat differently by subordinates, peers, and superiors. Each leader has critics and supporters. Each leader has a perception of him/herself which is influenced by the three groups—subordinates, peers, superiors—with which the leader works. The patterns appear to have some relationship to the sex of the leader (see Figure 7-1).

In one pattern the superior is most critical of the leader. Subordinates and/or peers, however, are strong supporters. The leader's self-conception is more similar to the view of subordinates and peers than it is of the more critical view of the superior. Jim Stevens, Paul Meyer and Dan Monroe exemplify this pattern with slight variations.

Jim Stevens and Paul Meyer have self-images which are similar to the way both subordinates and peers see them and both groups are supportive of these leaders. Dan Monroe, on the other hand, draws a profile of himself which is similar only to the way subordinates view him, and the subordinate group appears to be the only one which has a very favorable view of this leader. Hence these leaders appear to be identifying with the group of co-workers which offers them the most support and the most positive feedback. For the men working in larger organizations, Paul and Jim, subordinates and peers are the groups that offer the most support. The boss is the most critical. For Dan Monroe, working in a small organization, however, the pattern alters slightly. Here subordinates provide a supportive image of Dan, while his sole peer and his boss share a more critical view.

Figure 7-1

Patterns of Influence

Leader	Most Critical Group	Most Supportive Group	Most Like Self-Image
MEN			
Jim Stevens	superior	subordinates and peers	peers and subordinates
Paul Meyer	superior	subordinates	subordinates
Dan Monroe	superior and peer	subordinates	subordinates
WOMEN			
Carol Victor	peers	superior and subordinates	peers
Mary Duncan	peers	superior	superior
Eileen Grant	peer and subordinates	superior	superior

The patterns which emerge for the women are different in several ways. All three of the women described here receive their greatest *support* from their boss. In contrast to the men whose bosses are their greatest critics, these women exemplify the notion that a supportive boss is crucial to the success of women in management.

In *The Managerial Woman,* successful women executives describe their relationships with their bosses providing crucial support:

> The women likened him [the boss] to their fathers and described their relationship with him in similar terms. To each woman, he was her supporter, her encourager, her teacher and her strength in the company. He admired her competence and her will to — exceed . . . He believed that women should be in business and backed up this belief in his dealings with her, with other men in the company and with male customers and clients (Hennig and Jardim, 1977, p. 129).

Second, for two of the women, the peers are the greatest critics. In both of these cases, Mary and Carol, the peers also have the least positive attitudes toward women. Hence an additional consideration, attitudes toward women in management, appears to be relevant for women and not for men.

Third, the women follow the pattern of identifying most closely with the group that is most supportive—with one exception. For Mary Duncan and Eileen Grant, their self-image most closely matches the image drawn by their superior and strongest supporter. The exception, Carol Victor, sees herself as most like the image of her peers, her greatest critics.

Although Carol may be attempting to set herself up for advancement by identifying with the peer group (which is more critical) rather than her subordinates (who give her strong support) she is caught in a "double bind." Associating closely with subordinates would give her the support of positive feedback about herself as a leader, but would identify her with a lower status group. Associating closely with peers, however, gives her the status which is appropriate to her position, but may lead her to view herself as less competent. Carol's peers complain that she does not communicate adequately with them. She is understandably cautious in relating to this most critical group of co-workers.

These few examples are not meant to be conclusive evidence for the patterns of influence they illustrate. Nor are they meant to be exhaustive of the patterns which may exist in organizational life. These exemplary cases are rather meant to be suggestive of ways in which "the scene" changes when women are included in leadership positions.[1]

NOTES

1.   Furthermore, these examples serve to challenge some of the assumptions made about peer groups which were developed through studies of predominantly male work groups.   DeNisi and Mitchell (1978), for example, outline three "problems" with peer group ratings.   Each of these problems carries assumptions about the nature of peer groups.

The first problem cited by DeNisi and Mitchell is "friendship." The authors point out that friends usually give higher ratings to each other and that this tendency may bias peer ratings. Assumed is a cohesive and homogeneous group of friends/peers.

This assumption holds true for the two male leaders described in this chapter from large organizations.   Jim Stevens and Paul Meyer both belong to a peer group which is homogeneous or like them in terms of race, sex, and age.

The situation for women, however, is remarkably different.   First, the peer groups are not homogeneous. Second, for the women, the peer group is the most critical. In short, there is no evidence of a "friendship problem" in the peer ratings of these women.

The second problem cited by DeNisi and Mitchell (1978) is the problem of "sub-group effects."   The authors state their opinion that "Favoritism towards fellow sub-group members is a real problem in most settings."   For the same reasons described above, this assumption applies to men rather than to women. Women are more often marginal or token members of the sub-group of peers. As tokens they are subject to negative biases and more exacting performance standards rather then to favoritism.

The third and final problem cited by DiNisi and Mitchell (1978) is "stereotyping." The authors state that peer ratings have been shown to be stable over time.   This stability has been attributed to the tendency of peers to stereotype a new group member and to resist changing the stereotype once it is initially made. This problem too applies differentially to men and women.

The notion that peers stereotype each other is supported by the cases presented in this chapter. Both men and women are described by peers as having interpersonal styles consistent with sex characteristic stereotypes. The difference is that the male stereotypes are positively valued and the female stereotypes are negatively valued (see Chapter One).

CHAPTER EIGHT: LEADING AND LIVING IN THE FUTURE

"As we move into the 1980's, it becomes clear that the woman's movement has been merely the beginning of something much more basic than a few women getting good (men's) jobs. Paradoxically, as more women enter the workplace and share the breadwinning, their family bonds and values—human values as opposed to material ones—seem to strengthen."

Betty Friedan, *Feminism Takes a New Turn*

"The dominant forms of authority in our lives are destructive; they lack nurturance, nurturance—the love that sustains others—is a basic need, as basic as eating or sex. Compassion, trust, reassurance are qualities it would be absurd to associate with these figures of authority in the adult world. And yet we are free: free to accuse our masters that these qualities are missing."

Richard Sennett, *Authority*

Futurists are unanimous in predicting that the number of women entering the American workforce will continue to increase. A report from the United States Department of

Labor (1980) forecasts this trend with certainty—regardless of economic conditions:

> The most conservative projections through the 1980's forecast large increases in the labor force participation of women, especially those between the ages of 20 and 54. Even when assuming a low economic growth rate and a significant rebound in the birth rate (traditional barriers to women's employment), the Bureau of Labor Statistics expects participation of women 20 to 24 to increase to nearly 75 percent. Among women ages 25 to 54 (including the baby boom women), the low (no growth) estimate is over 70 percent during the 1980's. All indications are that women in the United States will continue to play an important and permanent role in the labor force.

The predicted increases do not mean that women will simply increase in numbers in female occupations, such as clerical workers. The predictions rather include an assumption that women will continue to expand the breadth and status of occupational choices available to them. New occupational frontiers will continue to open to female employees. In the news recently have been new opportunities in the military (Adams, 1980), politics (Shreve and Clemens, 1980) and the construction trades (U.S. Department of Labor, 1980, p. 13).

If these predictions are realized or partially realized, such an influx of women into formerly male domains will necessarily have an impact upon the culture of work organizations. The question of what kind of changes will occur is a matter of conjecture. The notion that women may "humanize" the workplace is highly controversial. In this Chapter I shall join the speculators and offer a scheme for viewing the alternative futures of women and men who lead.

ONE-WAY STATUS MIRRORS

One way of "getting a handle" on the kinds of changes which may take place as a result of women entering formerly male occupations is through the concept of "one-way status mirrors." James Beshers (1962), a sociologist, developed this term to describe what he saw happening to poor people in the cities who aspired to become middle class. The people in the lower-status group became preoccupied with the symbols of the higher-status middle class, such as Cadillacs and other big cars.

In their determination to obtain these status symbols for themselves, the people of the lower-status group failed to see that the values of the middle class were changing. By the time they bought their Cadillacs, the members of the middle class were driving Volkswagen Beetles. The lower-status Cadillac drivers had the desired symbol, but its value had changed. Hence they failed to obtain what they really wanted: middle-class status.

In Beshers' terms, the value of the symbolic Cadillac was manipulated by the higher-status group with the result that they, in their Volkswagens, were still obviously the elites. In the hierarchy of class, the value of the symbols was visible from above but not from below. Hence the metaphorical one-way status mirrors.

Two aspects of the one-way status mirrors concept are particularly salient to the case of women entering the ranks of leadership and other traditionally male occupations. One is that the values of status symbols are matters of interpretation. The other is that the correct interpretation of the value of symbols is highly classified information, available only to the higher-status group. Beshers (1962, p. 136) describes the function and importance of the values attached to status symbols.

> When an elite uses one-way visibility of symbols to help maintain its position, rather restrictive criteria are involved in the selection of appropriate symbols. The symbols must be either invisible or inconspicuous to the eye of the untrained observer. Inconspicuous symbols can be interpreted only by those who have

> received appropriate training, but this training must be monopolized by the higher classes or the lower class will be able to fake the symbols (Abbott, 1952) . . . a monopoly of both symbols and values must be maintained by a higher class in order to use a particular symbol to differentiate themselves from lower classes.

Hence, although a member of the lower-status group may attempt to "fake" a symbol by driving a Cadillac, for example, the higher-status group may respond by creating a "counter symbol," such as the Volkswagen Beetle.

When we consider behaviors to be status symbols, as Beshers does, then the one-way status mirror becomes relevant to the case of women in management and the issue of leadership styles. Should women be trained to act like men? To acquire the behaviors that symbolize the status of men's work?

The possibility exists that women will follow this path in seeking the status of leadership and men's jobs. Women may become so set upon the course of learning to act like men (in order to make it in a "man's world") that they may fail to see what is valued in leaders is changing. Books such as *Games Your Mother Never Taught You,* (Harragan, 1977), *Getting Yours,* (Pogrebin, 1975), and *The Women's Dress for Success Book,* (Molloy, 1977), have titles which—in spite of protestations of their authors to the contrary—imply that the way to success for a woman is to learn to act like a man. A common (mis)conception of assertiveness training and other women's leadership development programs is that they train women to act like men. Women are also "proving themselves" by demonstrating that they can accept corporate transfers ("Now Eager . . . ", May 26, 1980).

An explicit description of women eyeing the executive suite through one-way status mirrors comes from Warren Bennis (1980) in an article entitled "False Grit: The Myth that Says You've Got to be Macho to Get Ahead." The article suggests that women are emulating the behaviors of men at the same time that men are changing and creating behaviors that are counter-symbols. In Bennis' words:

What we see today are all kinds of workshops and seminars where women undergo a metaphorical sex change, where they acquire a tough-talking, no nonsense, sink or swim macho philosophy . . .Ironically, men are simultaneously encouraged to shed the same masculine character traits that women are trying to imitate through their own form of nonassertiveness and sensitivity training programs. So it's OK, even better than OK for old Charlie to cry in his office. How marvelous. How liberating. *Women impersonate the macho male stereotype and men impersonate the counter-macho stereotype of the woman"* (Bennis, 1980, p. 44, emphasis is my own).

Bennis goes on from this statement to conclude that we need to stop looking to individuals and sex role analyses to find ways of advancing the cause of women in management. He locates the problem in the organizational structures and cultures rather than in individual women in management. He asserts that organizations—not individual women or men—need to be transformed.

The essential point is that individual leaders can best be understood in the context of broader social issues and changes. (It is disappointing that many leadership studies discuss findings as if the subjects lived and/or worked in culture-free environments.) Furthermore, I propose that the concept of one-way status mirrors provides an illuminating focus for placing the twelve leaders described in the book into a broader social context. The concept also serves as a vehicle for projecting into the future and exploring the ways women and men may lead and live in years to come.

SHIFTING VALUES

Shifting values, an essential part of the one-way status mirror model, has been a recurring theme throughout this book. Part One began by asserting that behaviors which belonged to either a male or female stereotype seemed to be durable, but that the value—positive or negative—attached to the behaviors may be changing. Sensitivity, for example, may be becoming a positively valued trait in a leader, although this characteristic is part of the female stereotype. Furthermore, I noted that the male stereotype provided a *positive* standard against which leaders are evaluated. Female stereotypes, on the other hand, provide *negative* standards against which women are evaluated in leadership roles.

Taking a closer look at the twelve leaders suggested other ways that cultural values entered into the work lives of those women and men. In Chapter Three some of the so-called feminine traits—compassion, democratic rather than authoritarian processes—were positively valued in the milieu of the educational leaders. In this environment the image of the male leader was expanded to include these positively valued traits.

In the final chapter of Part I, two male and two female social service leaders were described. The organizational climate of their work included several attributes of the female stereotype: humanitarian values, a focus on process, the ability to listen empathically. In this environment we saw confusion and a breakdown of traditionally clear distinctions between male and female style.

In Part II, further evidence of confused and shifting values was found in examining the twelve leaders' self-perceptions. Comparing the leaders' self-perceptions with perceptions of co-workers, instances were found where an identical activity was described by both parties (leaders and co-workers) but assigned a different value. Eileen Grant, sales manager of a travel agency, for example, reported that one of her weaknesses as a leader was her tendency to jump in and take over when things went wrong. Eileen's co-workers also mentioned that when things went wrong she would "jump in and carry the ball." The co-workers, however, considered this tendency a strength.

In terms of the concept of one-way status mirrors this recurring theme of values—values shifting, values confusion, values redefinition—is part of women's status-seeking in the world of work. In simplified terms, as the men in power see women becoming competitive, as willing to disrupt their lives by accepting corporate transfers, and adopting many of the other ways which symbolize the status of men's work, they begin to shift the values attached to these status symbols.

The values confusion which is evidenced in the work lives of the twelve leaders presented in this book is a result of efforts on the part of the predominantly male leadership to maintain their position.   As women abandon their identity as the egalitarian sex, for example, the men in power adopt the counter symbol of participatory management.

A scenario of the future based on the notion of one-way status mirrors is a depressing future, depressing because there are no winners.   Women never gain the status they seek.   Male-dominated organizations are not able to benefit from their resources.   Daniel Yankelovich, a psychologist who has mapped changes in values during the past decade, talks about the unfortunate consequences of women's pursuit of "paid work" as a status symbol.

> Unfortunately, many women seem to have accepted unquestioningly the male-dominated values of the old era; instead of bringing men to a greater appreciation of the values of home, family, and child care, women have endorsed male values associated with paid work. (Yankelovich, 1978, p. 49).

A more optimistic scenario of the future results from rejecting the notion that women may be eyeing the executive suite through one-way status mirrors—a future in which masculine and feminine traits and activities are valued equally and employed according to what is functional rather than what is in power.   Betty Friedan expresses optimism about the future in stating:

> Paradoxically, as more women enter the workplace and share the breadwinning, their family bonds and values—human values as opposed to material ones—seem to strengthen. (Friedan, 1979).

Thus, to accept or reject the notion of one-way status mirrors is to cast a vote for a pessimistic or an optimistic future.   Whatever the future holds, it will be closely tied to the changing values of women and men.   I shall now discuss five issues which are key indicators of these changes:

achievement, family, leisure, the "macho" ethic, and andro-gyny.   While I shall not venture to predict the direction of change, the conflict and/or resolution of these issues will be critical to the futures of women and men as leaders.

TOPPING OUT, MIDDLE-AGED CAREER DROP-OUTS AND THE VALUES OF ACHIEVEMENT

The terms "topping out" and "middle-aged career drop-outs" refer to the phenomenon of women and men giving up successful careers and high ranking jobs for a different life style, a life style which includes fewer of the rewards, such as status and money, and fewer of the headaches, such as performance pressures, and long hours working at their successful careers.   The use of different words to describe the phenomenon for women and men is interesting.

In her article on topping-out in *Savvy: The Magazine for Executive Women*, (August, 1980, p. 28) Kathleen Fury states: "When a woman decides to abandon the rat race, it's called 'topping-out'.   When a man does it he's part of the new-values generation."   Ms. Fury is angry because the value of this symbolic behavior is changed.   She fears that the spectre of the woman as an uncommitted worker will be aroused by the woman who "tops out."   Employers may then use that old excuse for not hiring or promoting women.   Fury also reveals her own values: women should not do this because it looks as if they are not as tough as men.

The same subject is treated with a different values orientation in an article in *Business Week* (July 7, 1980).   The title, "Confident Enough to Drop Out", reveals the author's attitude of respect for those women (and men) who chose "freedom and lifestyle" over the "corporate ladder."   This article cites a study of female executive drop-outs that was conducted by a management counseling group:

> Preliminary   conclusions . . . indicate that women generally leave [high ranking jobs] for personal growth, freedom, the opportunity to be one's boss, and the chance to live a different kind of life—in brief, for the same reasons that men leave (p. 96).

Hence dropping-out is as respectable a choice for a woman as it is for a man.

FAMILY VALUES

I was once asked by a chemical company to conduct a study aimed at increasing the number of women working as chemical plant operators. At that time, the company employed five women out of one hundred operators. The job paid better than the "pink collar" positions, traditionally female clerical jobs of the company, and was a position that opened doors to advancement. Efforts to increase the numbers of women in these position had been plagued by high turnover.

The personnel officers of the company suspected harassment by male co-workers as the main reason why so many women did not stay in this position. They wanted me to investigate the question of what distinguished those women who were able to get through the hazing imposed by the male operators from those women who could not "take the heat" and quit. They hoped my study would define the strategies used to deal with such testing and harassment successfully.

A preliminary investigation on my part revealed the following facts about the job: Operators worked twelve-hour shifts, six days a week. Once signed on to a shift, an operator could not be called away from the job for any reason—not even a phone call.

I was five months pregnant with my second child at the time that this investigation took place, and wondered how any woman, or man, with a family could work under such conditions—with or without harassment from co-workers. When I proposed the projects to my young, "new values" students who were to conduct the interviews and observations of the female operators, one of their first comments was, "Has the company considered changing the hours of the job?"

Leadership roles are notoriously demanding in terms of time and energy. The accommodation of family and leadership roles is difficult to imagine outside of the traditional model of the woman doing all of the housekeeping and almost all of the parenting while the man does almost none of the parenting and all of the breadwinning. The twelve leaders described in this book are a case in point. Of the six men who participated in the study, five, or 83 percent, are married and have children. On the other hand, only two out

of six female leaders, or 33 percent are married.   Three of
the six women, or 50 percent, have children.   These figures
indicate that a greater conflict between family and leadership roles exists for women than for men.   Furthermore, in a
poll of sixty-six subordinates, peers, and superiors of the
leaders, thirty-nine, or 58 percent, thought that for a woman
to have both a career and children was too difficult.

One term used to describe the woman who adds the role
of career woman to the roles of wife and mother is "superwoman."   There is no male counterpart to the term, no
"superman" because men's families supposedly serve to
support their careers, not to make further demands on them.
But as Terborg (1977) points out in a review of the literature
on women in management, studies indicate that although it is
possible for women to assume managerial roles, it is difficult
for them to "shed" family roles.

The value attached to superwoman is shifty.   At one
time superwoman was positively valued she has lately come
into disfavor.   "The Superwoman Role is a Failure" declares
Ellen Goodman (*The Philadelphia Inquirer*, December 21,
1979).   In this columnist's words, the addition of the roles of
wife and mother to the role of career woman creates two
choices for women: "superdrudge or childlessness."   In an
article for *Savvy* (December, 1980) in which executive women
kept daily time logs, recording their activities from waking
up in the morning to bedtime, Ann Marie Cunningham reviews
these logs and concludes:

> As women take on many roles, we gain the
> considerable satisfaction of calling
> ourselves professionals or executives. We
> feel included in more parts of society. But
> we lose time and perhaps the inclination to
> think about exactly what we are doing. We
> work hard, but our work may add up to
> killing time. Forced to emphasize produc-
> tivity, we avoid that nasty worry about
> whether doing a lot equals achievement,
> whether having it all may mean losing it all
> (p. 52).

Other options, besides superwoman, for preserving
family values are possible. When asked how women might

combine careers and child rearing, 30 percent of people interviewed in this study felt that performing both roles at once, à la superwoman was too difficult. Most people in this group felt that women should have careers outside the home (93 percent of the 67 people asked the question, "In your ideal world would women have careers outside the home?") The solution offered by most people was that women drop out of the labor force for a period of time to bear and rear their children. Many people had very specific ideas of how long the hiatus for child rearing should be for a woman. Some said that a woman must stay at home until her children are in school, for others the age was third grade, still others said "through high school."

The six female leaders who participated in this study fit this pattern. The three women with children are older (ages 54, 56, and 59). All three had spent some years at home working as homemakers. The three younger women, on the other hand, had no children. Two of the three stated that they were undecided about whether they wanted children.

Although the older women were full of superwoman war stories, the younger women saw a conflict between having children and maintaining the momentum of a career. They seemed to share the opinion of scholars (Barrett, 1979; Rather, 1980) who reviewed strategies and results of nearly a decade of affirmative action programs around the world and concluded that the lack of continuity created by women dropping out to have children is one of the greatest causes of discrepant pay and job levels between women and men.

Another group of people in the leadership study (58 percent) responded to this question of how women might combine careers and children by suggesting that substantial changes need to be made in American life and work styles. Such changes would make it possible for women and men to "do it all." Most of the suggestions, when translated into organizational policy, concern some sort of alternative work schedule.

In their book on the topic, *Alternative Work Schedules*, Cohen and Gadon (1978) describe three alternatives to the normal forty (or fifty or sixty) hour nine-to-five work week. The first and most widely used to date is flexitime. An employee working on flexitime has some choice in determining what hours they will work. "Flexible working hours is essentially a work schedule that gives employees daily choice in the timing between work and non-work activities" (p. 33).

This arrangement of working hours has the potential of allowing parents to participate to a greater extent in the care of their children. Yet the first comprehensive study of flexitime indicates that parents spend no more time with their children than they did on a conventional work schedule. According to researcher Halcy Bohen:

> Though some flexitime advocates have hoped that flexible hours might increase husband's willingness to share family responsibilities with their wives, the study found few signs of such change . . . flexitime or no, working mothers still bear the primary responsibility for children, and most father still subscribe to traditional views of male and female roles ("Flexitime . . . ", August, 1980).

Another alternative work schedule described by Cohen and Gadon (1978) is the "compressed work week." "The compressed work week is a method for allowing a worker to accomplish 'full-time' work in less than the standard five (or more) day work week. By extending the length of the workday beyond the standard eight hours, a full week's worth of working time can be finished within three to four and one-half days, allowing for more than the usual two days off" (p. 49). This arrangement too has the potential for giving parents greater freedom to meet the demands of both work and family life.

The third alternative work schedule described by Cohen and Gadon (1978) is permanent part-time and job sharing. In both of these arrangements the employee works less than the regular number of hours required of full-time workers but has the status of a "regular permanent employee."

Another and final alternative to full-time employment for working parents is a "cottage industries" program which is being tried on an experimental basis by the Prudential Insurance Company. The program which is for women executives allows them to work at home while on maternity leave. The participants in the program pick up writing projects to be completed at home and returned to the office. The experimental project was viewed as a success by the company and is expected to expand (Kronholz, 1978).

THE VALUING OF LEISURE

A survey of the 1974 graduating class of Harvard's M.B.A. program indicated that income may be inversely related to happiness for graduates: Although the mean salary for the class was $46,000, the survey indicated "that the more money they [the graduates] were making, the unhappier they were. The factors that accounted for the low satisfaction were related to their families, general way of life and outside activities rather than to their jobs" (Ruch, 1980).

Several surveys have indicated that some members of the workforce are seeking a new balance between work and non-work time in their lives—especially younger workers. One such survey is reported by Cohen and Gadon (1978, p. 9): "blue collar workers, white collar workers, union members, the affluent, and professionals indicated a preference for long leaves, sabbaticals and shorter hours over other benefits" (*Roper Reports*, 1974). Thus the positive valuing of non-work time was expressed by a wide segment of the workforce, including the ranks of leadership.

In another survey by Yankelovich the importance of leisure in the "New Breed's" scheme of values is described:

> For the New Breed, family and work have grown less important and leisure more important. When work and leisure are compared as sources of satisfaction in our surveys, only one out of five people (21 percent) states that work means more to them than leisure (Yankelovich, 1978, p. 49).

THE MACHO MYSTIQUE

Fortune ran an article entitled "The Ten Toughest Bosses (Menzies, 1980)." The subtitle read: "A selection of corporate chieftains whose 'leadership is demonstrated when the ability to inflict pain is confirmed.'" Reading through this glibly written article it was difficult to discern the author's intent. Were these ten men being indicted for their inhumane ways, or were these tales of *machismo* a credit to these most demanding and unfeeling bosses? Finally, at the conclusion of the article the author points out the fact that keeping the ranks of followers filled with such a leader is problematic:

> It may very well be that a tough boss can attract and keep quality managers only as long as his methods keep making them winners . . . . When a company gets a reputation for high turnover, it becomes doubly hard to attract capable replacements.
>
> Of course, the revolving door also waits for the boss who fails. And when a tough boss fails, there are plenty of willing hands to help give that door a spin (p. 72).

A few weeks after the article appeared in *Fortune,* Robert Abboud of the First Chicago Corporation (one of the top ten) was fired. He was subsequently replaced by a man with a "distinctly" different style. The changeover was described in an article in *Business Week* (August 4, 1980):

> When the bank's board fired Abboud after his five-year reign, the reasons centered on the domineering and abrasive style that made Abboud banking's most controversial executive and that produced endless management turmoil and turnover. Sullivan [Abboud's replacement], a well-liked executive vice president of the Chase Manhattan Corp., has been deemed to have the "people skills" that Abboud lacked ("First of Chicago . . . ", 1980, p. 64).

In another article, "Europe Outgrows Management American Style" (Ball, 1980), a more clearly critical statement is made about American macho—through the eyes of European management. The opinion of one European company president is reported as "a greater inclination in the

U.S. to 'personalize' jobs, which shows up in the prevalence of domineering bosses and in the tendency when something goes wrong, to put in a new man rather than look for other factors affecting performance" (p. 148).

The article further reports that Europeans see American managers as "authoritarian" and "rank conscious" compared to themselves. They claim to be better at decentralizing and delegating authority than their American counterparts. The European view is that American managers do not practice what they preach about delegation of authority and collegiality. This is not just a question of *fashion* in management styles. The Europeans claim that the American macho style has significant negative consequences for individuals in terms of stifling initiative, inhibiting the recognition of talent, and for organizations in terms of adapting to "a rapidly changing business and social environment" (Ball, 1980, p. 148).

In addition to the difficulties of finding people who will work for the macho boss and of the maladaptive sorts of organizations the macho ethic tends to create is an even more serious indictment of *machismo*, "Nuclear Macho." In an article with this title, Ann Marie Cunningham, staff member of the President's Commission on the accident at the nuclear power plant at Three Mile Island, describes the sexual imagery used by the workers in the nuclear industry:

> Women remain on the periphery, away from the control room, where male technicians and engineers speak of the reactors as 'she.' At Three Mile Island, they talk of the day 'when she's back on line (operating normally) . . . and discuss what will happen 'if she goes critical'.
>
> Besides portraying technology as a woman who must be kept 'on line', nuclear machismo encompasses a certain swagger in the face of risks from radiation (Cunningham, 1980, p. 35).

Cunningham goes on to describe the work of "jumpers," the unskilled temporary workers hired by nuclear power plants for maintenance and repair operations. She talks about how these workers—men and women—accommodate the dangers of radiation exposure with the good pay and excitement of their work. She quotes one female jumper's "swagger" in the face of the possibility that exposure to radiation may cause cancer: "I have a funny attitude. I think people who worry about cancer get cancer. It's not going to get me, that's all" (Cunningham, 1980, p. 39). Another example of nuclear macho provided by Cunningham are the jumpers who remove their radiation measuring devices to avoid being laid off when the limit of exposure allowed by the Nuclear Regulatory Commission is reached.

Cunningham finally points out the strength of the nuclear macho ethic: "The average industry worker who questions nuclear machismo is up against a strong lobby that minimizes invisible radiation hazards: What you can't see can't hurt you. As the industry often says, 'where are the corpses we can point out?'" (p. 40).

The term macho was used in a similar context by Jimmy Carter in a presidential campaign address (Fall, 1980). In attacking his opponent's foreign policy, he stated that Ronald Reagan's "macho" attitudes could be dangerous for the United States, leading to a build-up of nuclear weapons and even war. He warned that for America to attempt under Reagan's leadership to be the "tough guys" of the world could lead to nuclear disaster.

ANDROGYNY

"Future space travel may be fraught with psychological hazards. The day of the macho test-pilot astronaut may be over" (Muson, 1980). The spaceship is an interesting psychological laboratory because both working and living occur in the same place. The National Aeronautics and Space Administration has been understandably interested in deriving a psychological profile of the person who could best withstand the stresses of confinement over a long period of time, such as on a long space mission. Results of a study to determine the best psychological make-up of future space flight crews indicate that the answer is "androgyny": ". . . the ideal astronaut may be men and women who score high on both instrumentality—a measure of the ability to manipulate the environment to achieve goals that is traditionally associated with 'masculine' men; and expressivity—a measure of emotional warmth and sensitivity to others that has always been considered a more feminine trait. Such people are usually labeled psychologically androgynous, though this does not tell us anything about their manner, appearance, or preference in sex or career roles" (Muson, 1980, p. 16). The rationale for this conclusion is that such people would at once be motivated to perform the required tasks (in their instrumentality) and also be able to get along with fellow crew members (in their expressivity) during a long period of confinement.

As futuristic as space travel, is author Alvin Toffler's (1980) prediction of a new "prosumer" work ethic. In essence, the people who live by this ethic will produce goods which they themselves will consume. Toffler sees the beginnings of this ethic in the self-help and do-it-yourself movements. He predicts that many people in the future may divide their time between part-time work in interdependent organizations and part-time work in small prosuming family units.

Toffler predicts that these changes in work patterns will lead to a redistribution of personality traits along androgynous lines:

> Today as more women are drawn into jobs producing for the market place, they, too, are increasingly objectivized. They are encouraged to 'think like a man'. Conversely as more men stay home, undertaking a greater share of the housework, their need for objectivity is lessened. They are 'subjectified'.
>
> Tomorrow as many Third Wave people divide their lives between working part-time in big, interdependent companies or organizations and working part-time for self and family in small, autonomous prosuming units, we may well strike a balance between objectivity and subjectivity in both sexes (Toffler, 1980, p. 28).

A more elaborate definition of masculine and feminine leadership and another call for androgyny comes from a conference of the National Organization for Women's Legal Defense and Education Fund. In a paper presented at this conference, Schwartz and Rosener (1980) define two styles of leadership, "alpha" and "beta." The alpha style—considered to be more masculine—is "based on analytical, rational thinking, relying on hierarchical relationships and tending to look for engineered solutions" (Nemy, 1980). The beta style, on the other hand, emphasizes "a concern for growth, learning and quality of life, with a long-range perspective that permits planning and an examination of different value choices" (Nemy, 1980).

Each style is considered appropriate under different circumstances. Each style is considered legitimate and is positively valued. Both styles are considered essential to resolving the so-called "leadership crisis" in America.

CONCLUSION

To summarize this discussion and return to the notion of one-way status mirrors, I shall use this last issue, androgyny, as an example. Considering the plight of men and women as leaders involves two separate and often confused issues, behaviors and values. A strong and recurring theme in American leadership literature is a dichotomy in leadership styles. Polarized styles have been called alpha and beta, male and female, instrumental and expressive, production-oriented and people-oriented, task and socio-emotional leadership, structure and consideration. Now there is strong evidence that values attached to these behaviors are shifting. To perceive a shift toward a more positive valuing of beta or stereotypically feminine leadership styles, however, does not necessarily mean an endorsement of women in management (although it does establish a climate in which women may more readily be perceived as suitable for leadership roles). The androgynous manager may, after all, be a compassionate *man*, a man with "people skills."[1]

In a similar way, however, the values attached to career achievement, family life, leisure activities and *machismo* may change, women may ever be the outsiders in terms of status. The notion of one-way status mirrors serves as a warning and a source of clarification. Sobering though this warning may be, it creates the opportunity for women to truly become leaders of equal status with men, to "blow their own horn" their own way rather than continuing to play the follower role, patterning themselves after male leaders in a dependent way. Perhaps women could assume a leadership role in humanizing organizations after all.

Toward a Richer Understanding of Leadership

A leadership crisis is being announced in America today at the same time that leadership scholars are throwing up their hands and declaring that for all of the studies of leadership we know almost nothing with certainty about this topic. Conferences of scholars are called with such titles as "Leadership: Where Else Can We Go?" and "Beyond Establishment Views." At these events (primarily) men who are leaders in their field irreverently declare that their favorite social science journal is *The New Yorker* (Vaill, 1978, p. 119) or a good novel (Sennett, 1980).

The warning of the one-way status mirrors applies to women in academe as well as to women breaking through into other fields. They can follow and try to fit themselves into the established male models of how research should be designed, conducted and reported. Or, they may follow their own instincts and chart new directions where their instincts conflict with existing, male-established norms. I shall sketch out here a few innovations that may be called feminist contributions to leadership research. They are feminist in the sense that they add beta-style (using intuitive, qualitative thinking) elements to the predominantly alpha-style (analytical, rational, quantitative thinking) of leadership research. Not all of the innovators are women although the majority are.

First is an *innovation in topic*, an effort to relate family life and leadership in the family to leadership in public and private organizations and political institutions. Kanter (1977) bridges the gap between work and family life through inclusion of the wives of executives in her book on *Men and Women of the Corporation*. Two books which take a psycho-historical approach to women as leaders focus on childhood family life as a determinant of participation in leadership roles in adult life. *The Managerial Woman* (Hennig and Jardim, 1977) discusses the families of corporate executive women. *The Making of Political Women* (Kelly and Boutilier, 1978) explores the primary families of political women. In a more profoundly psychological way, two efforts to relate the primacy of family life and early childhood to attitudes toward and manifestations of authority in public life are Richard Sennett's *Authority* (1980) and Dorothy Dinnerstein's *The Mermaid and the Minotaur* (1976).[2]

Second is an *innovation in the attitude of the researcher* towards the subjects of study. Smircich (1980) suggests the researcher adopt an empathic attitude toward subjects of study rather than the traditional neutral and objective posture. Two other authors take this a step further and express concern that the result of research be *useful* to the subjects of the study. Larwood and Lockheed (1979) make a plea for useful research because the women trying to "make it" in leadership roles urgently need answers. Weskott (1979) warns that women must avoid becoming mere objects (subjects) of research, a faddish topic of the "women's lib" era.

Third and finally are *innovations in reporting research.* Schreiber (1979) contends that methodological and procedural snags and doubts should be included in research reports. These important sources of information are traditionally hidden behind a macho facade of certainty and invulnerability. Other innovations in research reporting are women's studies journals that publish articles written in a style which is accessible to non-academics in an effort to bridge the gap between academe and the community.

Eugene Kennedy (1979) declares authority to be *the* issue of the 1980's. He states that although social science researchers have been preoccupied with the study of "authoritarianism," a "distortion of the use of authority," the concept of healthy authority has yet to be explored. Kennedy eloquently reminds us that "at its roots 'authority' does not mean *to control* but *to make able to grow,* suggesting the positive relationships parents have with their children, and authors have for their words and authorities for their judgments" (p. 112).

Reading through my notes from all of the interviews of the leadership study, including many descriptions of leaders, I am struck by the total omission of the word "nurturing" in reference to a leader. Yet many of the great mothers I have known have slipped easily into leadership roles outside the family, adapting the substantial leadership skills developed as leaders within the family. In a future world where workers expect greater self-fulfillment from their work and organizations are faced with a rapidly changing social and economic environment, we will need women and men who, as leaders, can nurture the human potential of their followers.

NOTES

1.   Dorothy Dinnerstein (1977) writes about the false hope attached to the androgyny concept.   She cites Norman O. Brown's "androgynous ideal of the unconscious" and poses this feminist critique: "this ideal emotionally androgynous humanity he (Brown) prescribess is still, physically and literally, *male* humanity.   In the world he evokes one does not sense the presence of ideally androgynous but physically *female* humans" (p. 184).

2.   Dinnerstein (1977) reminds us that as long as women are solely responsible for the care of young children, then everyone's first boss was a woman.

EPILOGUE

A follow-up questionnaire was sent to the twelve leaders of the study three years after the original contact with them was made. The purpose of the questionnaire was to track the progress of the leaders' careers and to assess the impact of changing societal conditions. Questions were asked about changes in jobs, working conditions, leadership styles, marital /family status, and status of women in their organizations. Eleven of the twelve leaders' questionnaires were returned.

Several themes emerged that relate to the questions raised in the last chapter: Are women eyeing the executive suite through one-way status mirrors? Training themselves to act like men at the same time men are changing their ways? How are values attached to the issues of topping-out, family, leisure, the macho mystique, and androgyny changing? What do these changes indicate about the warning that the notion of one-way status mirror implies?

First, what has happened to the individual leaders during the three years since the original study was conducted?

Jim Stevens, project director, is still employed by the same large corporation. No other information about his situation was available.

Carol Victor, project director, was promoted within her company. With this promotion she became more confident and more aware of the politics of her organization. She left her employer some time later to move with her husband to another state where she is studying to take the C.P.A. exam.

The travel agency owner has acquired a new branch office resulting in promotions for both of his sales managers. *Dan Monroe* is managing the new office on a profit-sharing basis. He reports that he supervises an entirely new staff that is smaller than his former staff. He is expected to make more policy decisions in his new position. In preparation for his new position he upgraded his credentials by achieving certification from the Institute of Certified Travel Agents.

With Dan out of the old office, *Eileen Grant* has been promoted to general manager. She reports that her new position is "more demanding" and has led her to become "more forceful" in her leadership style. Eileen also reports that she has acquired the divorce which was in the works three years earlier.

At the school district, *Paul Meyer* has been promoted to superintendent of a division in the district.   He is now responsible for 39,000 children in 11 schools. He has a new boss and more people and programs to supervise.   His new responsibilities include mediating personnel disputes and implementing the teachers' contract.   On a personal note, Paul reports that his son has married and he has become a new grandfather.

Mary Duncan has a new job title, increased responsibilities and more people and programs to supervise.   Her office has been moved to larger quarters.   This increased span of control makes her job more difficult and more "lonely"—as she no longer has time to be personally involved with each staff member.   Her family has also increased with the addition of two new grandsons.

Herb Weiss has the same position as department chairman at the university.   He reports that his leadership style has not changed although his job has become more difficult. The difficulty comes from a "new need for morale improvement among subordinates."

Rose Lerner still chairs her department at the university —a department which has grown to include both graduate and undergraduate programs.   This growth means that Rose now has a new graduate chairperson to supervise.   She reports that she is now more direct in "pointing out irregularities in the program to the faculty." Rose feels that in one way her job has become easier because of a new secretary who "can adapt very easily to participatory management." In another way the job has become increasingly difficult because of "bureaucratic requirements which seem to increase every year."

In the social services, *Joe Ryan* maintains his position as alcohol clinic director, but now has additional responsibilities and more involvement in the central administration of the mental health center. His job is entirely administrative now and he has hired a clinical director to supervise the counseling staff. The staff itself has changed from primarily part-time, non-professionals to entirely full-time professionals. Consistent with these changes, Joe has changed his style to become more directive, relying less on "processing." He has also learned to follow up verbal interactions with written memos. Joe feels that his job is now more difficult because of his role in the central administration, his new professional staff which demands more of him as a leader and because of an environmental factor, new federal and state regulations. These difficulties are manageable, however, because he has learned to better separate work and personal roles. A more detached posture allows him to work through difficulties on the job without too much personal stress. This represents an important achievement for Joe because he feels that vulnerability to stress at work contributed to the termination of a long-term personal relationship with a woman.

Susan Baker has resigned her position as clinic director to seek new challenges and because she felt that her pay increases were not keeping pace with increases in responsibilities (more programs and supervisees). Susan reports that the administrative nature of her job forced her to learn to delegate, to detach herself from her work and to use a secretary more efficiently. Her leadership style became more confident, "more forceful," "hesitating less," "questioning her own authority less."

Ron Smith remains in his position as director of the criminal justice agency with a staff that is reduced in size. Economic pressures have made his job more difficult, forcing him to "be more critical in judging staff production" and "to give more time to fund raising." This economic pressure is the overriding influence on Ron's job.

Finally, *Anna Ferrari's* criminal justice agency has closed down because of lack of funds. She has been working part-time as a consultant and is looking for full-time employment.

Perhaps the most obvious of the themes that emerged from the comments of the leaders is a *difference in job stability between the women and the men.* One-half of the women left their employers of three years ago and a fourth woman, Rose Lerner, was planning to "step down" from her chairperson role—yet remain at the university. By comparison, none of the men (including Jim Stevens who did not return his questionnaire) had made a move. Furthermore, only one of the men was even in the market for a change in employer.

Reasons for leaving their jobs differed for each of the three women concerned. Anna Farrari's criminal justice agency had closed down because of a lack of funding. Carol Victor had, after a promotion, resigned her position as project director at a large private corporation in order to move with her husband to another state. Susan Baker had resigned her position as director of the alcohol clinic for a complex of reasons: 1) Her responsibilities had increased while her salary had not; 2) Her job was becoming increasingly administrative with less opportunity for Susan to be an educator and a therapist; 3) She wanted "new challenges." Rose Lerner wants to be freed of administrative responsibilities in order to have more time for research and writing.

Elements of topping out are evident in these women's career decisions. While not as dramatic as the Wall Street lawyer who moved to a small town in the southwest ("Confident Enough . . . ", 1980), three of these women are questioning the (assumed) automatic climb up the organizational ladder. Carol Victor put family values first and relocated with her husband. Susan and Rose found that their administrative positions did not leave them time for the activities they enjoyed the most. They put these preferences ahead of the power and status of their administrative roles.

Another theme which runs through the leaders' comments is *the pressure of "rough times" for the American economy.* The leaders in the social service agencies, the public school system, and the small business all reported this "pressure." Different leaders responded differently to the change in economic conditions.

Eileen Grant saw the situation as a challenge of "improving on a project or goal that has been deemed a failing market." She reports that her leadership style has changed "to become more forceful and determined." She now insists on greater productivity from employees. The pressure has created a "swing toward togetherness" among her employees.

Both Paul Meyer and Mary Duncan as administrators for the school district report the pressure of declining resources. To Paul this development makes his job more difficult, makes him "highly accountable" for his decisions and actions. For Mary, the scarce resources created a struggle to make new quarters for her enlarged staff into a comfortable place to work. She describes her "fight." "This [move to new quarters] took the ability to negotiate with many different departments since the move came at a time when budgets were strained and my boss didn't do too much to assist. One of the department heads in another department who helped me to get the place painted and get air conditioners said he'd do it for me since I had helped his department many times by running a series of supervisory development courses for three years on a continuous basis for all of his people—some one thousand or so."

Economic pressures have, however, been most acutely felt in the criminal justice agencies. The agency directed by Anna Ferrari closed because of inadequate funding.   Ron Smith reports significant changes in his job because of "funding problems."   The number of staff members has been reduced.   Hence Ron has "had to be more critical in judging staff production."   He has had to reassess his priorities and devote more of his own time to fund-raising activities.   In short, economic conditions have made his job more difficult.

Clearly, the pressures of rough times promote so-called "macho" styles of leadership, influencing leaders to become more production-oriented, tougher, more aggressive.   Eileen Grant swaggers in the face of this challenge: "What is expected of me is only the beginning of what I have to offer in my position."   Carol Victor describes the "considerable backstabbing" and the "great competition and scramble for the few managerial slots open" in her company.   Even Paul Meyer who criticized himself in the original study for those times when the pressures of work made him too production-oriented, is now concerned about accountability.

Another force influencing the leaders to adhere to the macho mystique is the structure of the upper-level management jobs into which they are being promoted.   Another theme which runs through the leaders' comments is *an increase in responsibility and span of control leading to increase in emotional detachment from work and subordinates, the use of a directive style, and unilateral decision-making.* Paul Meyer, in his new job as superintendent of a district serving 39,000 children, describes a change in his decision-making process: "I tend to incorporate the broadest base of opinion or concern, but the time frames are shorter and decisions are reached with far less discussion."   Joe Ryan, clinic director, describes a similar decrease in "processing with staff" and a shift to a "more directive" leadership style.   Joe's fellow clinic director, Susan Baker, reports that she is "still basically process oriented but not so 'religious' about it."

Another theme—related to the promotions—is the observation that *the leaders were promoted whether they like it or not.* Paul Meyer's description is neutral, matter-of-fact. He describes himself as simply shifting styles to accommodate his new position. To Joe Ryan the changes are definitely "positive," indicating "professional development" and "maturity."

Two of the women, however, have mixed emotions about their increased responsibilities and the consequent changes in style. Mary Duncan eloquently describes her feelings about supervising a larger, more diverse staff at the school district:

> It's a more lonely job in many ways because I can't be a 'buddy' and a boss. With a small staff as it was several years ago and with all women I still had to be the boss but there there didn't seem to be the need to discipline as much. Now with a man on my staff and several young instructors who seem not to be as disciplined personally themselves, I have to keep a little distance . . . . Supervising more people and having more programs requires one to be more careful not to let people just "pop in" my office. I try to be a good leader and give people the time they need but also have time for my own work too— or I find myself taking too much work home nights and weekends.

In a similar way, Susan Baker describes the process of weaning her alcohol clinic staff from her direct supervision as she moves up to assume administrative responsibilities on a state level. "The difficulty in all of the above [her move up in the organization] was prioritizing and finishing—but mostly keeping everyone happy—teaching the alcohol staff to expect less direct contact with me, accept more responsibility themselves and benefit from the 'wider' responsibility I was taking. This was difficult but I'm sure some days we all wanted the 'good old days'."

A final theme that runs through the comments of these leaders is *the opinion that the status of women in the organizations is improving.* Project Director Victor expresses the opinion that in her company there is "more acceptance of women and growing recognition that women can be relied upon to be tireless and dedicated workers." At the school district, Paul Meyer reports his sense "that a greater percentage of new principals are female," and Mary Duncan cites the establishment of a new office dedicated to promoting equal opportunity for women. Herb Weiss states that women at his university have received promotions and that he is "learning how best to use appropriate vocabulary with women." Clinic Director Ryan reports that, while the number of women in the central administration has not changed, the women hired recently are different: "younger than the original staff, more assertive and informed about womens' issues." Finally, Susan Baker observes that at her clinic the ratio of men to women among department heads has shifted. Formerly, there were five men and three women. Now there are five women and three men; hence in terms of numbers of women holding leadership positions and their acceptance in these roles, these workplaces have become more androgynous.

In conclusion, the three-year development of these leaders provided little evidence for the notions that women are learning to be like men or that men are changing very much. The careers of the men, rather, indicate that they readily succumb to the pressures of economic hard times and the demands of upper-level management positions to become directive, detached, production-oriented leaders à la macho mystique. The women, on the other hand, raise more questions on the way up: Can I do what I really want to do in this job? Is moving up the only way to find a change, new challenges? Is this job compatible with my family needs and responsibilities? Is it worth it? The future of America's leadership crisis may lie in our organizations' willingness and ability to respond to these questions.

APPENDIX A: INSTRUMENTATION

Leader Behavior Description Questionnaire

The two subscales of the revised Leader Behavior Description Questionnaire—form XII (L.B.D.Q.) which were used in this study are Role Assumption and Initiation of Structure. Each subscale consists of ten statements about the leader of a work group. Each item begins with the pronoun "He" (or "She") and describes a specific behavior that a leader may enact.

Respondents are instructed to decide how frequently their leader engages in a particular behavior and to select one of five possible responses: always, often, occasionally, seldom, or never. The instructions emphasize that responses should be descriptive rather than evaluative.

In scoring the questionnaire, each item receives a score value that can range from five to one—or one to five for negatively stated items—as shown in the following examples:

He/she lets group members know what is expected of them.

Always (5) Often (4) Occasionally (3) Seldom (2) Never (1)

He/she fails to take necessary action.

Always (1) Often (2) Occasionally (3) Seldom (4) Never (5)

The score for each subscale consists of the sum of the scores obtained on the items of the subscale divided by ten, the number of items.

While reliability and validity measures are higher when all twelve subscales of the instrument are used together, subscales have been used separately with reliability measures which indicate sufficient stability for research purposes (Stogdill and Coons, 1957).

Construct validity of the subscales has been demonstrated by a factor analysis of the subscales. Results of this study indicated that "Each subscale exhibited a high loading (between .71 and .96) on a separate factor. With one exception, no two subscales were highly loaded on the same factor.

These results suggest that each factor is defined by a separate subscale" (Stogdill, Goode and Day, 1963).

Interpersonal Adjective Check List

The Interpersonal Adjective Check List was originally developed as a diagnostic tool with psychiatric populations. The instrument has been used productively, however, in studies of organizational behavior.[1]

The Interpersonal Adjective Check List is a paper and pencil instrument that was developed by LaForge and Suczek (1955) from an observation system by Leary (1957). According to Leary, "The chief concept employed . . . is the interpersonal mechanism which is defined as the interpersonal function of a unit of social behavior. The rater or observer asks the following question: What is the subject of the activity, i.e., the individual whose behavior is being rated, doing to the object or objects of the activity? The answer, e.g., he/she is aggressing against them, affiliating with them, teaching them, etc., is the interpersonal mechanism."

The system consists of sixteen categories which are organized around two dimensions: dominance-submission and hostility-affiliation. Each category is a combination of these dimensions, e.g., "supporting" is seen as a combination of "affiliation" and "dominance." The instrument also has an intensity dimension.

The Check List consists of 128 items—eight for each of the 16 interpersonal variables. Each of the sixteen variables is represented by a four-point intensity scale. "For each variable there is one intensity 1 item, which reflects 'a mild or necessary amount' of the trait. Three items refer to intensity 2, 'a moderate or appropriate amount' of the trait. Three words reflect intensity 3, a 'marked or inappropriate amount' of the trait. And one word expresses intensity 4, 'an extreme amount' of the trait (Leary, 1957, p. 455).

An example of the items for variable "dictatorial" consists of the following:

1. Able to give orders
2. Forceful
   Good leader
   Likes responsibility
3. Bossy
   Dominating
   Manages others
4. Dictatorial

The Check List is administered in alphabetical order. The respondents are instructed to indicate which items are descriptive of the person he/she is rating.

Scores are obtained by summing the items checked for each variable. A style profile for each subject consists of the series of scores on each of the sixteen variables. Since the variables are also viewed as eight conceptually similar variables, data may be collapsed into octants; in each case a profile will be a series of eight scores. Or, scores on the octants may again be combined to form scores on the four dimensions: dominance, hostility, submission, and affiliation.

Reliability and construct validity have been established at levels sufficient for research purposes, and are reported by Leary (1957).

Because the 128-item Check List was to be included with other instruments in the questionnaire, a shortened version was considered to be necessary for use in this study. Therefore, a version containing 64 items, one-half of the original 128, was developed.

Women as Managers Scale

The Women as Managers Scale (WAMS) was developed by Peters, Terborg and Taynor (1974) to assess attitudes toward women assuming managerial positions in business. The instrument was adapted for use in this study by adding the word "supervisors" to the items wherever the word "managers" was used. Also, the term "business community" was changed to "work community." The purpose of these changes was to generalize the instrument for use in other than business organizations.

The scale consists of 21 items. Each item makes an attitudinal statement about women and managerial work, e.g., "In general, challenging work is more important to men than it is to women." Respondents are instructed to rate each item on a seven-point scale: 1 = strongly agree, 2 = agree, 3 = slightly agree, 4 = neither agree nor disagree, 5 = slightly disagree, 6 = disagree, and 7 = strongly disagree. The instructions emphasize that responses should be based upon "personal opinion."

In scoring the WAMS, each item receives a score value that can range from seven to one, or one to seven for negatively stated items, as shown in the example below:

It is acceptable for women to compete with men for top executive positions.

Strongly Agree (7), Agree (6), Slightly Agree (5), Neither Agree nor Disagree (4), Slightly Disagree (3), Disagree (2), Strongly Disagree (1)

It is not acceptable for women to assume leadership roles.

Strongly Agree (1), Agree (2), Slightly Agree (3), Neither Agree nor Disagree (4), Slightly Disagree (5), Disagree (6), Strongly Disagree (7)

The score for each scale consists of the sum of the scores obtained in the 21 items.

Reliability measures of the WAMS clearly suggest that it meets the requirements of stability necessary for research purposes. Supportive evidence also exists for the construct validity of the WAMS. These results are reported by Peters, Terborg and Taynor (1974).

The Interview

An interview was developed to provide a measure, in addition to the WAMS, of the subjects' attitudes toward women. With the exception of one question, the interview was adapted from an attitude survey of the Women's Action Program, United States Department of Health, Education, and Welfare (Loring and Wells, 1972). In addition to the questions on attitudes toward women, one question was included about the leaders: "How would you describe _____'s strengths and weaknesses as a leader?" The purpose of this question, like the questions on attitudes toward women, was to add a subjective dimension to the objective measures of role legitimation included in the questionnaire.

The questions were ordered from easier to more difficult or from less personal to more personal. The interview was designed to be conducted in one-half hour, and seven questions in all were included:

1. How would you describe _____'s strengths and weaknesses as a leader?

2. What are some difficulties you've experienced with women supervisors? Can you remember a situation that was particularly difficult?

3. What are some difficulties you've experienced with men supervisors? Can you remember a situation that was particularly difficult?

4. What things have helped men and women to advance in this organization? Are they different for men than women?

5. How have the new laws on equal employment opportunity for women affected your career?

6. What differences have you observed in the ways that men and women work?

7. In your ideal world, would women have careers outside the home? How would they combine the careers with marriage? With children?

NOTES

1. Two examples of applications of the Interpersonal Adjective Check List appear in: a) Tagiuri, et al., (1968) and b) Jones and Pfeiffer (1977).

Interpersonal Check List Profile Sheet

Octant	I	II	III	IV	V	VI	VII	VIII
Totals								

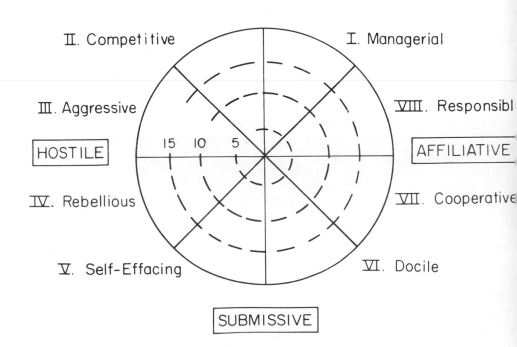

A leadership training program, described below, was developed as an application of the findings of the leadership study and as a way of making the kind of feedback provided by the interpersonal style profiles available to others. The course was designed to meet once a week for a two-hour session, and to continue for six weeks. Participation was limited to twenty persons.

The announcement of the course read as follows:

Lady Bosses Don't Have To Be Bitchy

This course is based upon the notion that women don't become successful leaders by trying to act like men. The course is designed for any woman who has or aspires to have managerial or supervisory responsibilities. The course would be useful to women who have supervisory responsibilities on the job as well as to homemakers who manage household and family.

The focus of the course is on developing a leadership style that is both feminine (comfortable for you) and effective. Common pitfalls and strengths of female supervisors will be examined. Each participant will have the opportunity to develop her own style profiles—both real and ideal. Opportunities will be provided for each participant to try out her ideal style in the supportive atmosphere of the class.

First Session

The first meeting begins with a warm-up exercise, leadership interviews. The interviews provide a vehicle for participants' getting to know each other and an orientation to the *introspective* and *change* foci of the course. Participants are asked to find a partner and interview each other using the following interview schedule.

183

1. What is the context or situation in which you lead or would like to lead?

2. How did you get to this position?

3. What did you consider to be the strengths and weaknesses of your leadership style?

4. Where do you see yourself going in your career? What are your ambitions? What changes would you like to make in your leadership style? What new skills would you like to develop?

After each participant has had a chance to play both the roles of interviewer and interviewee, partners introduce each other to the group as a whole using the information gathered during the interviews.

The leadership interviews take up a major part of the time allowed for the first meeting. After this warm-up a mini-lecture is given on the role theory model of leadership. The significance of sex stereotypes in the role episode and women's particular vulnerability to role conflict are emphasized (see Chapter One). After questions and discussion of the model the meeting is adjourned.

Second Session

The second meeting begins with a brief review of the role episode model and the function of sex stereotyping. Participants are then invited to "tune in" to their own stereotypes or images of male and female leaders. Instructions are given to write down characteristics of male and female authority figures they have known or characteristics they would expect to find in a female or male boss. After about five minutes instructions are given to review the list and record a "+" or "-" for characteristics which are positively or negatively valued respectively.

Composite male and female images are then developed for the group as a whole by listing the characteristics—with their value signs—on a blackboard or newsprint. A discussion of the composite then follows. The discussion may include a comparison of the class's composites with the images of the leadership study (see Chapter One). Differences due to the passage of time or to the particular backgrounds of the participants may be covered in the discussion.

The second class meeting concludes with a look at the twelve style profiles from the leadership study. Individual profiles are compared and contrasted to the stereotyped images of male and female leaders developed earlier. As each pair of profiles is presented, the provocative question may be posed: Which profile represents a female leader? Which represents a male leader? Discussion of how the individual leader's profile relates to and deviates from the stereotypes follows.

Third Session

The third meeting is devoted to administration of the Interpersonal Check List and the development of leadership style profiles. A brief formal introduction to the instrument is first given. The introduction includes information on the developers and development of the instrument and the assumptions about personality underlying the construction of the instrument (see Appendix on Instrumentation).

Following this mini-lecture on the Interpersonal Check List participants are given materials for the administration and scoring of *two* profiles. Instructions are given to mark one checklist "real" and to complete it by marking those items which describe the participant in a specific leadership role—real or hypothetical. The second check list should then be marked "ideal" and completed by marking those items which describe the participant as he or she would *ideally* behave in that same leadership role. The two check lists are then self-scored by the participants.

When all or most of the participants have completed the scoring of their real and ideal leadership style profiles, they are asked to find a partner with whom they could comfortably work. Partners are then instructed to share with each other the profiles they have just developed, focusing on differences and similarities between the real and the ideal and on defining specific behaviors or situations that illustrate the profile and its interpretation. At this point I like to emphasize that there is no "correct" interpretation of the profiles and that their usefulness will be greatest for those who can concretize them by relating them to specific things that they do in the leadership role in question.

After the pairs have had some time to interpret and discuss the profiles, participants are invited to share interpretations and reactions with the group as a whole. Finally, the suggestion is made to solicit feedback from co-workers (subordinates, peers, or superiors) through administration of the check list. Extra copies of the check list and scoring sheets are provided for this purpose. The session is adjourned with a request to bring all profiles to the next meeting.

Fourth Session

The fourth session begins with reporting in on "homework." Participants are invited to report on their experiences administering the check list to others and/or discovering behavioral patterns that illustrate the profiles.

After this introduction participants are asked to return to the partners with whom they had worked at the last meeting. With this partner they are to develop goal statements based on the information provided by the profiles. The goal statements should be as *specific* as possible and phrased in the form of "I want to be able to . . ." or "I want to be . . .." Examples of goal statements that have been developed in the Lady Bosses course are: "I want to be able to run the show and still be friendly." "I want to be able to delegate without fearing for my standards and reputation," and "I want to be ambitious without being cut-throat."

Following the development of goal statements, the activity, role playing, is introduced. The following process may be used:

1. One of the participants presents a goal statement to the class and describes an example, drawn from their work life, of the undesirable behavior. The goal is then clarified and, if necessary, scaled down to workable dimensions.

2. The participant selects class members to play supporting roles and enacts the "scene" from their work life.

3. Brief discussion of the role play is held.

4. Another class member replays the role, changing the undesirable behavior and demonstrating the desirable behavior as defined by the goal statement.

5. (optional) Another class member enacts the role, demonstrating yet another way or style of achieving the same goal.

6. Finally, the participant whose goal is on stage, re-enacts the role, changing the undesirable behavior in line with her own goal.

7. Discussion of the entire role play may follow. Time permitting, another role playing sequence is undertaken.

Fifth Session

Session five begins with a brief report on "homework." Participants may be asked if—in light of the week's events— insights concerning the interpretation of the profiles emerged, or if changes in goal statements are in order, or if they have experimented with new behaviors. "Strokes" are awarded accordingly.

The remainder of the session is devoted to role playing. The process begun at Session Four is continued with the goal of allowing each participant to enact a role. In a larger group this may be accomplished by dividing the participants into several smaller groups which would work simultaneously.

Sixth Session

The final session is devoted to future planning and evaluation. The session begins with participants returning to the partners with whom they have worked in previous sessions. With their partner they are asked to reassess their goal statements, to redefine, clarify, and verbalize the goals with their partner.

In the group as a whole, then, participants are invited to share goal statements in their final form.

Following the reassessment of goals, a "brainstorming" session is held to develop ideas for follow-up activities. Some of the follow-up activities which have been suggested are: "doing a self-appraisal with the check list regularly," "sharing my goals with a friend," or "with my superior," "posting the goals," "having another meeting of this group in six months," and "doing some reading on the topic, assertiveness."

After the "brainstorming" has generated a number of ideas, participants are instructed to return to their partners to develop a personal plan of action. The plan should be verbalized to the partner, and put into writing as well.

The final session ends with a course evaluation. I have used the following items to solicit feedback:

1. The *most* useful activity or part of this course was . . .
2. The *least* useful part of this course was . . .
3. The leader's strengths and weaknesses were . . .

INTERPERSONAL CHECK LIST [1]

Directions for the following sixty-four items

a.   READ each item carefully.

b.   THINK about whether the item describes the leader as you know him/her.

c.   DECIDE whether the qualities described by the item are a TRUE (T) or FALSE (F) description of the leader.

d.   DRAW A CIRCLE around one of the two letters (T F) following the item to show the answer you have selected.

T-True

F-False

e.   MARK your answer as shown in the example below.

Example: It is true that he/she is "considerate"
Example: It is false that he/she is "easily fooled"

1.	Always pleasant and agreeable	T F
2.	Appreciative	T F
3.	Agrees with everyone	T F
4.	Admires and imitates others	T F
5.	Able to give orders	T F
6.	Apologetic	T F
7.	Able to criticize self	T F
8.	Bitter	T F
9.	Businesslike	T F
10.	Bossy	T F
11.	Cooperative	T F

12. Can complain if necessary . . . .   T F

13. Can be strict if necessary . . . .   T F

14. Distrusts everybody . . . .   T F

15. Dictatorial . . . .   T F

16. Dominating . . . .   T F

17. Encourages others. . . . .   T F

18. Eager to get along with others . . . .   T F

19. Easily fooled . . . .   T F

20. Egotistical and conceited . . . .   T F

21. Easily embarrassed . . . .   T F

22. Friends all the time . . . .   T F

23. Frequently disappointed. . . . .   T F

24. Firm but just . . . .   T F

25. Frequently angry . . . .   T F

26. Forceful . . . .   T F

27. Generous to a fault. . . . .   T F

28. Gives freely of self . . . .   T F

29. Helpful . . . .   T F

30. Hard to impress. . . . .   T F

31. Hard-hearted . . . .   T F

32. Hardboiled . . . .   T F

33. Impatient with others' mistakes . . . .   T F

34. Independent . . . .   T F

35. Kind and reassuring . . . .   T F

36. Lets others make decisions . . . .   T F

37. Modest . . . .   T F

38. Overprotective of others . . . .   T F

39. Often helped by others. . . . .   T F

40. Often admired . . . .   T F

41.	Obeys too willingly	T F
42.	Passive and unaggressive	T F
43.	Respected by others	T F
44.	Spoils people with kindness	T F
45.	Spineless	T F
46.	Shy	T F
47.	Stubborn	T F
48.	Slow to forgive a wrong	T F
49.	Skeptical	T F
50.	Straightforward and direct	T F
51.	Self-seeking	T F
52.	Shrewd and calculating	T F
53.	Somewhat snobbish	T F
54.	Self-reliant and assertive	T F
55.	Self-respecting	T F
56.	Too lenient with others	T F
57.	Too easily influenced by friends	T F
58.	Trusting and eager to please	T F
59.	Thinks only of him/herself	T F
60.	Tries to be too successful	T F
61.	Very respectful of authority	T F
62.	Wants everyone to like him/her	T F
63.	Will believe anyone	T F
64.	Will confide in anyone	T F

NOTES

1. This shortened version of the Interpersonal Check List is adapted from the original instrument of LaForge and Suzcek (1955). The complete, original instrument is described by LaForge (1977; 1973). The ICL is excluded from copyright protection and may be reproduced without special permission for any legitimate research use.

Directions for Scoring the Interpersonal Check List—

A) For each item that is marked "true" record the appropriate number of points in the appropriate octant or column on the profile sheet.

B) Add up the total number of points for each octant.

C) Shade in the portion of each octant that represents the total score for that octant. (Each octant or pie slice represents a total of 20 points.)

D) Add up the scores for octants 1 and 2, 3 and 4, 5 and 6, 7 and 8 to create the four quadrant scores, dominant, hostile, submissive, and affiliative.

		OCTANT NO.	POINTS
1.	Always pleasant and agreeable	7	2
2.	Appreciative	6	1
3.	Agrees with everyone	7	4
4.	Admires and imitates others	6	2
5.	Able to give orders	1	1
6.	Apologetic	5	2
7.	Able to criticize self	5	1
8.	Bitter	4	3
9.	Businesslike	2	2
10.	Bossy	1	3
11.	Cooperative	7	1
12.	Can complain if necessary	4	1
13.	Can be strict if necessary	3	1
14.	Distrusts everybody	4	4
15.	Dictatorial	1	3
16.	Dominating	1	3

		OCTANT	NO. POINTS
17.	Encourages others	8	2
18.	Eager to get along with others	7	2
19.	Easily fooled	6	3
20.	Egotistical and conceited	2	4
21.	Easily embarrassed	5	2
22.	Friends all the time	7	3
23.	Frequently disappointed	4	2
24.	Firm but just	3	2
25.	Frequently angry	3	3
26.	Forceful	1	2
27.	Generous to a fault	8	3
28.	Gives freely of self	8	2
29.	Helpful	8	1
30.	Hard to impress	4	2
31.	Hard-hearted	3	4
32.	Hardboiled	3	2
33.	Impatient with others' mistakes	3	3
34.	Independent	2	2
35.	Kind and reassuring	8	2
36.	Lets others make decisions	6	3
37.	Modest	5	2
38.	Overprotective of others	8	3
39.	Often helps others	6	2
40.	Often admired	1	2
41.	Obeys too willingly	5	3
42.	Passive and unaggressive	5	3
43.	Respected by others	1	2
44.	Spoils people with kindness	8	4

		OCTANT	NO. POINTS
45.	Spineless	5	4
46.	Shy	5	3
47.	Stubborn	4	3
48.	Slow to forgive a wrong	4	3
49.	Skeptical	4	2
50.	Straightforward and direct	3	2
51.	Self-seeking	3	3
52.	Shrewd and calculating	2	3
53.	Somewhat snobbish	2	3
54.	Self-reliant and assertive	2	2
55.	Self-respecting	2	1
56.	Too lenient with others	8	3
57.	Too easily influenced by friends	7	3
58.	Trusting and eager to please	6	2
59.	Thinks only of him/herself	2	3
60.	Tries to be too successful	1	3
61.	Very respectful of authority	6	2
62.	Wants everyone to like him/her	7	2
63.	Will believe anyone	6	4
64.	Will confide in anyone	7	3

BIBLIOGRAPHY

Abbot, E., *Flatland.* New York: Dover Publications, 1952.

Adams, V., "Jane Crow in the Army: Obstacles to Sexual Integration." *Psychology Today,* October 1980, p. 50.

"All Male Clubs: Threatened on All Sides." *Business Week,* August 11, 1980, p. 90.

Ball, R., "Europe Outgrows Management American Style." *Fortune,* October 20, 1980, p. 147.

Barrett, N. S., "Women in the Job Market: Occupations, Earnings and Career Opportunity," in R. E. Smith (ed.) *The Subtle Revolution: Women at Work.* Washington, D.C.: The Urban Institute, 1979, 31-61.

Bateson, M. C., *Our Own Metaphor.* New York: Knopf, 1972.

Bartol, K. M. and Wortman, M. S., Jr., "Sex of Leader and Subordinate Role Stress: A Field Study." *Sex Roles,* 5(4), 1979, 513-518.

Bennis, W., "False Grit: The Myth that Says You've Got to be Macho to Get Ahead." *Savvy,* June 1980, p. 43.

Bernstein, P. W., "Upheaval at Bendix," *Fortune,* November 3, 1980, 48-56.

Beshers, J., *Urban Social Structure.* New York: The Free Press of Glencoe, 1962.

Bowman, G. W., Worthy, N. B. and Greyser, S. A., "Are Women Executives People?" *Harvard Business Review,* 43, 1965, 12-18.

Bradford, D. L., Sargent, A. G. and Sprague, M. S., "The Executive Man and Woman: The Issue of Sexuality." In F. E. Gordon and M. H. Strober (eds.), *Bringing Women into Management.* New York: McGraw-Hill, 1975.

Broverman, K., Vogel, S. R., Broverman, D. M., Clarkson, F. E., and Rosenkrantz, P. S., "Sex-Role Stereotypes: A Current Appraisal," *Journal of Social Issues, 28*(2), 1972, 59-78.

Chernesky, R. H., "A Guide for Women Managers: A Review of the Literature." *Administration in Social Work, 3*(1), Spring, 1979.

Cohen, A. R. and Gadon, H., *Alternative Work Schedules: Integrating Individual and Organizational Needs.* Reading, Massachusetts: Addison-Wesley, 1978.

"Confident Enough to Drop Out." *Business Week,* July 7, 1980, p. 96.

Cunningham, A. M., "Nuclear Macho: Swagger in the Face of Radiation Risks." *Savvy,* August 1980a, p. 34.

Cunningham, A. M., "The Time-Pressured Life: A Look Into the Diaries of Superwoman." *Savvy,* December 1980b, p. 38.

Day, D. R. and Stogdill, R. M., "Leader Behavior of Male and Female Supervisors: A Comparative Study." *Personnel Psychology, 25,* 1972, 353-360.

DeNisi, A. S. and Mitchell, J. L., "An Analysis of Peer Ratings as Predictors and Criterion Measures and a Proposed New Application." *Academy of Management Review,* April 1978, 369-374.

Dinnerstein, D., *The Mermaid and the Minotaur.* New York: Harper Colophon Books, 1976.

Ezell, H. F., Odewahn, C. A. and Sherman, J. D., "Being Supervised By a Woman: Does It Make a Difference?" In R. C. Huseman (ed.), *Proceedings of the Academy of Management,* Detroit, Michigan, August 1980.

Fasteau, M. F., *The Male Machine.* New York: McGraw-Hill, 1974.

Fiedler, F. E., "A Note on Leadership Theory: The Effect of Social Barriers Between Leaders and Followers." *Sociometry, 20,* 1957, 87-94.

"First of Chicago: New Management to Bring Back the Past." *Business Week,* August 4, 1980, p. 64.

"Flexitime Does not Flex Family Time." *Psychology Today,* August, 1980, p. 20.

Fowler, E. M., "A Survey on Women Directors." *The New York Times,* October 7, 1977, p. D5.

Friedan, B., "Feminism Takes a New Turn." *The New York Times Magazine,* November 18, 1979, p. 40.

Fury, K., "Mentor Mania: The Search for Mr. Right Goes to the Office." *Savvy,* January, 1980a, p. 42.

Fury, K., "Topping Out: What Happens When You Deliberately Derail Your Career? *Savvy,* August,1980b, p. 24.

Galbraith, J., *Designing Complex Organizations.* Reading, Massachusetts: Addison-Wesley, 1973.

Goodman, E., "Superwoman Role a Failure." *The Philadelphia Inquirer,* December 21, 1979, p. 13-A.

Greenstein, T. N., "Behavior Change Through Value Self-confrontation: A Field Experiment." *Journal of Personality and Social Psychology, 34,* 1976, 254-262.

Gross, N., Mason, W.S., and McEachern, A. A., *Explorations in Role Analysis: Studies of the School Superintendency Role.* New York: Wiley, 1975.

Harragan, B. L., *Games Mother Never Taught You.* New York: Rawson Associates, 1977.

Hammer, S., "When Women Have Power Over Women." *Ms. Magazine,* September, 1978, VII, (3), p. 49.

Hasenfeld, Y. and English, R. A., *Human Services Organizations.* Ann Arbor: University of Michigan Press, 1977.

Heller, G. M., *A Comparative Study of Women and Men in Organizational Leadership Roles.* Doctoral Dissertation, Temple University, 1978.

Heller, T., "When Women Emerge as Leaders in a Group, Task and Maintenance Roles are Combined." Unpublished paper, 1977.

Henning, M. and Jardim, A., *The Managerial Woman.* New York: Anchor Press/Doubleday, 1977.

Homans, G. C., *The Human Group.* New York: Harcourt, Brace and World, 1950.

Howard, S., *But We Will Persist: A Comparative Research Report on the Status of Women in Academe.* Washington, D.C.: American Association of University Women, 1978.

Hoy, W. K. and Miskel, C. G., *Educational Administration: Theory, Research and Practice.* New York: Random House, 1978.

Huse, E. F., *Organization Development and Change.* St. Paul: West Publishing Company, 1975.

Jones, J. E. and Pfeiffer, J. W. (eds.), *The 1977 Annual Handbook for Group Facilitators.* La Jolla, California: University Associates, 1977.

Jourard, S. M., "Some Lethal Aspects of the Male Role." In J. S. Pleck and J. Sawyer, (eds.). *Men and Masculinity.* Englewood Cliffs, N.J.: Prentice-Hall, 1974.

Jourard, S. M. and Richman, P., "Disclosure, Output and Input in College Students." *Merrill-Palmer Quarterly of Behavioral Development, 9,* 1963, 141-148.

Kahn, R. L., Wolfe, D. M., Quinn, R. P., Snoek, D. J., and Rosenthal, R. A., *Organizational Stress: Studies in Role*

Conflict and Ambiguity. New York: John Wiley and Sons, 1964.

Kaiser, R. B., "The Georgia on L.A.'s Mind." *The New York Times Magazine,* December 23, 1979, 22-26.

Kanter, R. M., *Men and Women of the Corporation.* New York: Basic Books, 1977a.

Kanter, R. M., "Women in Organizations: Sex Roles, Group Dynamics, and Change Strategies." In A. G. Sargent, *Beyond Sex Roles,* St. Paul: West Publishing Company, 1977b.

Kanter, R. M., "Why Bosses Turn Bitchy." *Psychology Today,* 9, May 1976, 56-89.

Katz, D. and Kahn, R. L., *The Social Psychology of Organizations.* New York: Wiley, 1966.

Kelly, R. M. and Boutilier, M., *The Making of Political Women.* Chicago: Nelson-Hall, 1978.

Kendall, K. A., *Reflections on Social Work Education 1950-1978.* New York: International Association of Social Work, 1978.

Kennedy, E., "The Looming 80's." *The New York Times Magazine,* December 2, 1979, p. 68.

Kerson, T. S. and Alexander, L. B., "Strategies for Success: Women in Social Service Administration." *Administration in Social Work,* 3(3), Fall 1979.

Kirschenbaum, H. and Simon, S. B., "Values and the Futures Movement in Education." In A. Toffler (ed.), *Learning for Tomorrow: The Role of the Future in Education.* New York: Vintage Books, 1974, 257-271.

Kronholz, J., "Management Practices Change to Reflect Role of Women Employees." *The Wall Street Journal,* September 13, 1978, p. 1.

LaForge, R., "Interpersonal Check List" in J. E. Jones and J. W. Pfeiffer (eds.), *The 1977 Annual Handbook for Group Facilitators.* La Jolla, California: University Associates, 1977.

LaForge, R., *Using the ICL.* Unpublished technical report, 1973. (Available from Rolfe LaForge, 83 Homestead Boulevard, Mill Valley, California 94941.)

LaForge, R. and Suczek, R. F., "The Interpersonal Dimension of Personality III: An Interpersonal Check List." *Journal of Personality, 24*(1), 1955, 94-112.

Larwood, L. and Lockheed, M., "Women as Managers: Toward Second Generation Research." *Sex Roles, 5*(5), 1979, 659-665.

Laurent, A., Managerial Subordinacy: A Neglected Aspect of Organizational Hierarchies." *Academy of Management Review, 3,* (2), April 1978, 220-230.

Leary, T., *Interpersonal Diagnosis of Personality.* New York: Ronald Press, 1957.

Levinson, D., *Seasons of a Man's Life.* New York: Knopf, 1978.

Lewin, K., *Field Theory in Social Science.* New York: Harper, 1951.

Lindsey, K., "Sexual Harassment on The Job: How to Spot It and How to Stop It." *Ms. Magazine,* November 1977, p. 47.

Loring, R. and Wells, T., *Breakthrough: Women Into Management.* New York: Van Nostrand Reinhold, 1972.

Maccoby, E. E. and Jacklin, C. N., *The Psychology of Sex Differences.* Palo Alto: Stanford University Press, 1974.

Mann, R. D., "A Review of the Relationships Between Personality and Performance in Small Groups." *Psychological Bulletin, 56*(4), 1959, 241-270.

Menzies, H. D., "The Ten Toughest Bosses." *Fortune*, April 21, 1980, p. 62.

Miner, J. B., "The Managerial Motivation of School Administrators." *Educational Administration Quarterly*, 1968, 4, 55-71.

Molloy, J. T., *The Woman's Dress For Success Book*. New York: Warner Books, 1977.

Muson, H., "The Right Stuff May be Androgyny." *Psychology Today*, June 1980, p. 14.

Myers, S., *Every Employee a Manager*, New York: McGraw-Hill, 1970.

Nemy, E., "'Male-Female' Leadership Discussed." *The New York Times*, October 31, 1980, p. A20.

"Now Eager to Accept Transfers." *Business Week*, May 26, 1980, p. 153.

Ohio State Leadership Studies and the Bureau of Business Research. Leader Behavior Description Questionnaire —Form XII, Columbus: Ohio State University, 1962.

O'Leary, E., "Some Attitudinal Barriers to Occupational Aspirations in Women." *Psychological Bulletin, 81*(11), 1974, 809-826.

Osborn, R. N. and Vicars, W. M., "Sex Stereotypes: An Artifact in Leader Behavior and Subordinate Satisfaction Analysis?". *Academy of Management Journal, 19*, September 1976, 439-449.

Peters, L. H., Terborg, J. R., and Taynor, J., "Women as Managers Scale (WAMS): A Measure of Attitude Toward Women in Management Positions.: *JSAS Catalog of Selected Documents in Psychology, 4*, 1974, 27.

Pogrebin, L. C., *Getting Yours: How to Make the System Work for the Working Woman*. New York: Avon Books, 1975.

Powers, T. E., "Administrative Behavior and Upward Mobility." *Administrator's Notebook, 15,* 1964, 1-4.

Ratner, R. S., "Equal Employment for Women: Summary of Themes and Issues." In R. S. Ratner (ed.), *Equal Employment Policy for Women,* Philadelphia: Temple University Press, 1980.

Rokeach, M., *The Nature of Human Values.* New York: The Free Press, 1973.

Rokeach, M. and McLellan, D. D., "Feedback of Information About the Values and Attitudes of Self and Others as Determinants of Long-term Cognitive and Behavioral Change." *Journal of Applied Social Psychology,* 1972, *2,* 236-251.

Roper Reports. "Work, Desires, Discontents and Satisfactions." June 1974.

Ruch, R., "Humanizing the MBA." *The Chronicle of Higher Education,* May 27, 1980, p. 56.

Sennett, R., *Authority.* New York: Knopf, 1980.

Schein, V. E., "Relationships Between Sex Role Stereotypes and Requisite Management Characteristics Among Female Managers." *Journal of Applied Psychology, 60,* June 1975, 340-344.

Schein, V. E., "The Relationship Between Sex Role Stereotypes and Requisite Management Characteristics." *Journal of Applied Psychology, 57,* April 1973, 95-100.

Schreiber, C. T., *Changing Places: Men and Women in Transitional Occupations.* Cambridge, Massachusetts: The MIT Press, 1979.

Schwartz, P. and Rosener, L., "Women in Leadership in the 1980's." Paper presented at a roundtable discussion of the NOW Legal Defense and Education Fund, October 1980.

Shapiro, E., Haseltine, F. P. and Roe, M. P., "Moving Up: Role Models, Mentors and the 'Patron System,'" *Sloan Management Review, 19*, Spring 1958, 51-58.

Shingledecker, P. and Terborg, J. R., "Employee Reactions to Supervision and Work Evaluation as a Function of Subordinate and Manager's Sex." Paper presented at the 40th Annual Meeting of the Academy of Management, Detroit, Michigan, August 1980.

Shreve, A. and Clemans, J., "The Rise of Women in Politics." *The New York Times Magazine*, October 19, 1980, p. 28.

Smircich, L., "The (Mis)Management of Meaning." Working paper, 1980.

Spector, A. R., "Mentoring, Womentoring and More." Paper preented at the 40th Annual Meeting of the Academy of Management, Detroit, Michigan, August 1980.

Stogdill, R. M., *Handbook of Leadership: A Survey of Theory and Research.* New York: The Free Press, 1974.

Stogdill, R. M. and Coons, A. E., *Leader Behavior: Its Description and Measurement.* Columbus: Ohio State University, 1957.

Stogdill, R. M., Goode, D. S., and Day, D. R., "The Leader Behavior of Corporation Presidents." *Personnel Psychology, 16*, 1963, 127-132.

Szakacs, J., "Survey Indicates Social Work Women Losing Ground in Leadership." *NASW News, 22*, April 1977, p. 12.

Tagiuri, R. L., et al., *Behavioral Science Concepts in Case Analysis.* Cambridge: Harvard University, 1968.

Terborg, J. R., "Women in Management: A Research Review." *Journal of Applied Psychology*, 1977, *62*(6), 647-664.

Thomas, E. J. and Biddle, B. J., "Basic Concepts for the Variables of Role Phenomena." In B. J. Biddle and E. J.

Thomas (eds.), *Role Theory: Concepts and Research,* New York: Wiley, 1966, 51-63.

Toffler, A., "A New Kind of Man in the Making." *The New York Times Magazine,* March 9, 1980, p. 24.

U.S. Department of Labor, Office of the Secretary, Women's Bureau, *Employment Goals of the World Plan of Action: Developments and Issues in the United States, July 1980.*

Vaill, P., "Toward a Behavioral Description of High-performing Systems." In M. W. McCall, Jr. and M. M. Lombardo (eds.), *Leadership: Where Else Can We Go?,* Durham, N. C.: Duke University Press, 1978, 103-125.

Weick, K., "The Spines of Leaders." In M. W. McCall, Jr., and M. M. Lombardo, (eds.), *Leadership: Where Else Can We go?,* Durham, N. C.: Duke University Press, 1978, 37-61.

Weskott, M., "Feminist Critique of the Social Sciences." *Harvard Educational Review,* 49,(4), November 1979, 422-430.

Yankelovich, D., "The New Psychological Contracts at Work." *Psychology Today, 11,* (12), May 1978, p. 46.

INDEX